WITHDRAWN

# College Talks

# College Talks

by
Howard F. Lowry

EDITED BY JAMES R. BLACKWOOD

New York
OXFORD UNIVERSITY PRESS
1969

To

# CURT TAYLOR

Office of the President

# Preface

In 'The Fifth Year,' President Lowry of The College of Wooster laid some ground rules for a baccalaureate. The first rule for the speaker, he said, is this: 'Realize that not all you say will be heard.' But much of what President Lowry said was heard and is remembered—remembered, what's more, with a growing sense that his life had embodied the things he said; so that these pages are not the weary, year-end rumblings of an ulcered administrator, but, in a real sense, a zestful account of 'the mind's adventure.' President Lowry felt that the purpose of education is 'not to dull or take the edge off the things we care most deeply about, the things we have loved and the causes we've served, but to put even them in the enriched and heightened relationships.' He did so in his college talks.

These talks drew from President Lowry his own best utterance of himself. He struck this triad: intelligence, clarity, and warmth. Many gifts fused in 'a particular singleness, an unusual wholeness' of thought and speech, and 'a certain grandeur' rose out of his desire to say clearly *one* thing worth remembering. Naturalness and humor lit up his talk with an apparently easy grace that had cost him hours, indeed years, of work. Whatever eloquence is, he had it. Yet those who heard him, year after year, tend to think of his timing and technique, his flowing style and the ripples of anecdote and wit, as altogether secondary, and recall primarily what it was he most wanted to say.

Now and then President Lowry plucked a talk straight from

the headlines. For convocation or baccalaureate, however, his thoughts grew slowly from the universal themes that are said to characterize the best literature of our time: the journey, isolation, struggle, the search for innocence or integrity, the paradox of life-in-death. He remarked that the most difficult part of any talk was deciding on a particular theme or symbol. For the listener, any symbol he chose to illuminate was likely to be as unpredictable beforehand as it would be memorable afterward. In looking back, of course, one can trace the beginnings to the merest phrase, repeated, echoed through the years, and at last amplified to the full scale of baccalaureate Sunday: 'the big world,' 'the transformed journey,' 'the not so lonely crowd,' and 'values and sanctions' among others. President Lowry had a prolific mind; he did not often repeat himself. Yet he had lived a long time with the thoughts given voice in this book.

These pages have been edited. All but two of the addresses are baccalaureates. Most of the introductions are shorter than they originally were. Some (not all) of the 'family talk' has been omitted; a few (not many) of the longer passages have been condensed or cut. A snatch of poetry or a one-line quip, if used in various contexts, may appear in only one. President Lowry's lifelong battle with gadgets is mentioned, though not so often as he mentioned it. His final salute to 'the ladies and gentlemen' of the senior class was different each year; but he nearly always closed with the same words, 'The Lord bless you and keep you. . . .' These words to the seniors are printed in 'The Apprentice's Secret,' his last baccalaureate at Wooster.

One purpose of *College Talks* is to keep a faithful record of the postwar era, now largely gone, in American education; another, deeper one is to see and lay to heart one man's vision of 'what was, and is, and will abide.'

*Winter Haven, Florida*                                    J. R. B.
*February 1969*

# Contents

# College Talks

# The Mind's Adventure
## (1944)

Last Wednesday afternoon we observed to our entering class that this College was dedicated to the glory of God and to humane learning. We asked some re-dedication to the latter. A Christian college is more than a Sunday school; it is an institution of high learning. If it invites young men and women to its fellowship, it must not deceive them. It must not offer them a pious fraud, but an education based on first-rate scholarship, warmed and enlivened by fresh research and the constant play of the creative imagination. Ever sensitive to what Henry More once called the rise and fall of life in the soul of man, it must, at the same time, give to its students an education that competes with the best offered by secular colleges and universities. A college that lives off stale platitudes and minor pieties, that conducts a four-year witch-hunt on small matters while dodging or ignoring the great realities of our common life and the splendors of the human spirit, is a traitor to its trust and is not dedicated even to the glory of God. It is not in spite of Wooster's being a Christian college, but because it is one, that we want it to be distinguished for humane learning.

Yet at the heart of Wooster—the deep source from which it draws its life—is a clear (to some a preposterous) commitment.

And we who have come here to complicate our minds, do well to remember what it is. This College holds that behind all life is a great and loving Father who works through man, who gave man the free choice of good and, therefore, the possibility of evil; who exacts justice but loves mercy; and who, through the sheer miracle of love, gave His only begotten Son that man might have everlasting life. The logical result of any such belief is evangelical Christianity. It has to be, because evangelical Christianity is the only kind of Christianity there is. The mark of the true follower of Christ is (1) a desire to change his own life and to better his own practice, and (2) to see such change in the lives of others.

And here may I speak very frankly to those of you who are not, perhaps, yet sure of what you do believe. The fellowship of Wooster certainly includes you—covets you, in fact. And we shall try, I hope, to play fair with you. We want to give you the chance to discover your own ideas and to allow the silent growth of the loyalties within your blood. We shall never, in our class-rooms, withhold from you any fact because it is hard or embarrassing or unpleasant. We shall not hurry you to throw about great words like 'truth' and 'spirit' and 'salvation'; for such words should always rise authentically from the convictions of your own mind and heart. We shall not offer you a debased religion that is pure spasm, or set any 'spiritual bear-traps' for you, such as the eighteenth-century poet James Beattie set for his child when he planted cress in the garden so it would come up to spell the child's initials, and thus, through the argument from design, persuade him to a proper faith in the divine order.

But, on the other hand, you must not resent it if Wooster wants you to be a Christian and to accept, in your mind and heart, the great fundamentals of the Christian faith. Any place once touched by Christianity has to feel that way—otherwise it's a complete fake in terms of itself. It is human nature's own bent to want to share the things that matter to it. One of the deepest forms of human loneliness is the loneliness of seeing great beauty and grandeur by oneself—scenery, music, painting, and famous historical places. There is something acutely miserable about coming on a fine passage in a book without being able to hand it at once to all your best friends. In like manner, a man who has once felt the power of Christ to make all things new in his own life, anyone who, after some failure of his own to live up to his best, has felt God's mercy and its re-creative force, has an instinct to go at once to his friends, that they may share in it, too. All this has, of course, its own law of good taste—but the passion it represents, the passion of friendship, is one of the first fruits of any Christian living. Properly tempered with humor and self-forgetfulness, it is not a mean but a noble thing.

Nor, in inviting you to an adventure in Christianity, will Wooster assume that Christianity is something that can necessarily be studied—any more than one can make a person moral, as it has been said, by spraying him two hours a week with a course in ethics. In a sense, Christianity cannot be studied at all. It is a laboratory experiment, and you have to try living it with what power you can summon, if you want to know what it is. John Hunter, the great eighteenth-century physician and scientist, always asked his research students, 'Have you performed the experiment?' Weary of dissection and ready to rush to unfounded hypotheses, they always heard Hunter's sharp rebuke, 'Gentlemen, do not think; try and be patient.' So Wooster summons you not merely to a life of Christian thought, but also to a life of Christian action. It does not ask you, either, to escape the world, but to draw, as you can, from the spiritual world that which floods the physical world and transforms it. It asks of you some of those great creative renunciations that lie at the heart of Christian ethics—not that your lives may be thin and meagre, but that they may be fulfilled. Frankly, we shall invite you to prayer and, as more than one man has learned, for a very simple reason—that Christ, who was the great expert in these matters and whose insight went deeper than any man's of whom the world has record, prayed; and it seems at least a fair proposal to follow His example if we are to know, for ourselves, the things He knew.

Now all this is very shocking to some secular educators. They say they have no dislike for Christianity—though I recall Dr. Flexner's reminder of the captain in Lord Nelson's navy who said, 'My Lord, I have no prejudices, but God knows I hate a Frenchman.' Liberal education, they say, cannot sully itself with religion and philosophy—with things that lead to commitment. Such things, they say, involve the emotions and a whole array of feelings that are pure dynamite. During the past two years I have listened to more than one institution debate its future policy. They all know that education today stands convicted of one cardinal sin—multiplicity of means and poverty of ends and general purpose. We have multiplied discovery on discovery, fact upon fact, gadget on gadget—with no more general sense of deep satisfaction than the world has today in the face of its own tragedy for having done precisely the same thing. Above all, education, if it is to have any order or meaning, must brood on one great question: 'What is man?' A hard question, involving the whole human activity—the intellect, the will, the emotions. Little wonder there is temptation to dodge it and enchant ourselves with things and mere empirical knowledge. Many institutions do dodge it—under one good pretext or another; either that, or they give it a purely intellectual or historical treatment, gingerly holding the eternities at arm's length between thumb and finger. They permit students to develop unrelated specialities and learn all manner of bright tricks without any over-all purpose or directing belief whatsoever. One of my own students, last term, put it to me straight: 'You ask us what we want after this war? We want an education that, by the end of sophomore year, has at least raised for us the questions worthy to be asked by a man. The answers are another matter. But we'll settle for nothing less than an education concerned with the total implication of things. We are tired of heaped-up fragments. All this is our right as men.' I thought it a fair request. Paradoxically enough, a university that cuts short the mind's adventure is really not a university at all. What I love about Wooster (and the cause of my deepest joy at returning here) is that it allows to education the full human adventure—the search for an understanding of what man really is in the light of the full powers of man—the intellect, the emotions, the will, and (if I may add) the deep quietness at the center where we hear the inner voice that comes at last, if we listen carefully, to teach us all, the voice that has spoken to anyone who has ever learned anything very much worth knowing.

There is, of course, a defense of Christian education as liberal education on very practical and secular grounds. Three great cultures—the Greek, the Roman, and the Hebrew—have formed the Western world. Why be ignorant of one of the three? How far can one go in art, in music, in literature, in history, in social thought, without a knowledge of the Bible and the great documents of the Church? One of the poverties of our contemporary mind is our lack of common symbols for expressing our great ideas. Part of this poverty came with the decline of classical learning and with the advent of anthologies of English literature in which Zeus and Apollo have to be annotated and painfully described as if they were something wanted by the government, and a simple phrase like 'pater noster' has actually to be translated. We experience a similar poverty from our religious illiteracy. Slowly the great secular books which have used these symbols for nineteen hundred years are closing to men who cannot read them with any ease or pleasure. Moreover, there is a matter of common honesty here. Men who would never think of pronouncing upon secular matters without consulting the sources and the prime authorities, easily conclude about Christianity without examining the evidence—the Old and New Testament. There are very few vagaries of college students that one, with a little time and patience, cannot understand. But there is one that has always stumped me completely. Why is it that students who will sit up far into the night talking about the philosophy of religion or the psychology of religion are content to remain in almost abysmal ignorance of the Bible, which is the great original document in these matters? In no other department of learning would such flimsy research procedure be even tolerated.

Such are the secular grounds for including religion in any liberal education. But the real ground is better still—for only through such study does the mind of man complete its human adventure.

This adventure is, among other things, an adventure in profundity—the profundity that consists, not in impressive learning, but in the effort to retain perspective—in the effort to keep a few fundamental ideas constantly checking on the rest of the mind's activity. These ideas are the pillars of philosophy—or the pole stars, if you will, by which we steer. They cut across red tape, order our confusion, and let fresh air blow through our speculations. Let me illustrate. Alexander Meiklejohn, the distinguished ex-president of Amherst, has written a three hundred-page book in which he seeks to find a decent principle for all higher education. With more learning than most men can summon, he deplores the fade-out of Christianity. He tells us, however, that some hope is left. The guiding star of all future education will be Humanity (with a capital H)—an idea of universal brotherhood that every teacher will serve. Yet nowhere in his learned book does Dr. Meiklejohn raise the one simple fundamental question that any child would want to know: Who fathered all those brothers?

Another example. We probably face no more depressing fact in our philosophy than the awful waste of Nature. How, amid this terrible fecundity, can I think of individual man or even man as a class—as marked for special distinction—let alone as a creature little lower than the angels and crowned with glory and honor? 'Twenty-one civilizations,' says Arnold Toynbee, 'are recognized by the historian, of which fourteen have already disappeared entirely.' The scientist can count more than two million species, of which man is one. Depressing data. But wait for the voice of the philosopher cutting through to first principles. And here it comes. 'Yes, this is all very discouraging,' says MacNeile Dixon. 'But we have one important point yet to consider. If man is but one of two million species, he still has this great distinction. He is, as far as we know, the only one of the two million who has ever been depressed by the fact.' What would you say, if urged, is the chief intellectual defection of our time? I think I should say it is our general neglect of the idea of the First Cause. Behind our mass of facts and our empirical data there are still the ancient questions—Why? How? By whom? In our busyness, our pride of discovery, our learning, we forget these lodestar questions that, difficult though they may be to answer, do keep our minds straight and deliver us from hopeless superficiality. These questions are the stock in trade of philosophy and religion.

They keep alive in us, also, the great sources of wonder that ought to form—and so rarely form—our estimate of life. To me, one of our real problems arises from the fact that all the really impressive things which happen to us, generally take place in our experience very early and become trite before we ourselves have become reflective beings. By the time we are ready to form our philosophy of life, we are thoroughly accustomed to the miracles of love and pity, the beauty of holiness, the grandeur of sacrifice, the sky, the earth, and sea. All the great and noble parts of man and earth are, by that time, common and often jaded material. But suppose you were Plato's man coming from your dark cave to your full faculties and were then allowed what you and I too seldom have—the fresh, unspoiled view of elementary things. Suppose it were the first afternoon of the world and the shadows began to form, and darkness began to stride across the land, and the sun go down. What a miracle it would be to you if, in a few hours, that the sun should rise—and on the other side of the earth. In fact, if anybody dared prophesy, in the first great twilight, that the sun would rise, you would execute him on the spot as a 'wishful' thinker. Yet, having once seen the returning dawn, with the full faculties of the mind, when would you forget it?

There is a quiet, elementary way—a great original way of looking at things—that is the basis of all right thinking. The presence
in our minds of the leading questions raised by philosophy and
religion keeps those full faculties for the discovery of truth alive.
'They make us,' as one says, 'the friends and companions of the
images of wonder.'

The mind's adventure that is born of religion will never permit
us, moreover, to take that jaunty view of the world that is a frequent mark of the modern temper—the view that morality is all
relative to time and place, changing with the customs of tribes
and peoples. How many a man, when things get a little rough for
him, begs to be excused from certain of our culture-conquests on
the ground that the Eskimos think otherwise about it—and
what's good enough for the Eskimos is good enough for him. Let
us grant that there are mores and 'conventions' wrongly inflated
to the rank of morals; but there is another perverse tendency in
us—to write off as 'mores' and 'conventions' whatever is difficult
for us as morals. Samuel Butler, the seventeenth-century satirist,
condemned the Presbyterians:

> Who condone the sins they are inclined to
> By damning others that they have no mind to.

If we look firmly at the matter, we discover that the moral alarm
clock is probably better marked and better set than we think; the
problem is really the problem of what to do when it rings. Surely
the mind sensitive to religious values knows that there are truths
and commitments living in the depths of our being—truths to
which, as Pascal said, we have no title, but to which we are
bound for ever. Jonathan Edwards—what a hard head he had!—
used to say 'there are things in this world that are more than intellect and more than feeling. They are pure supernal light! ' One
of my favorite passages in all literature is that remarkable insight
of Bishop Wilson's—'The joy of righteousness is so great that it
would be a kind of debauchery—were it not so difficult.'

Christianity is not merely an adventure in profound and adequate ideas. It is an adventure in freedom. Free choice is at the heart of the Christian conception—man given the dignity of choosing good and evil that he may have the honor of free commitment, the honor of being not a puppet but a person. 'The gift of God is eternal life' one of my old teachers used to remind me out of the New Testament; and what is the very essence of a gift?—the fact that we don't have to accept it. A desperate choice, given to us at the total risk of ourselves. Little wonder that so many of our English liberties go back to those men in the seventeenth century who took political freedom as a simple matter of course, a deeper, original freedom already being theirs at so great a wager. Such freedom creates that automatic respect for personality out of which democracy thrives. We can preach tolerance at home and hold international conferences abroad till the end of time, and all our work will be in vain unless men of good will possess the world—men who value themselves as immortal persons bought at a price, and who, thus valuing themselves, value other persons also. This is the mind's adventure in brotherhood that follows the mind's adventure in true freedom.

All liberal education is, finally, an adventure in humility. And so, in the final adventure of the liberal mind, he learns again the wisdom of the humble. He first loses his life and then he finds it again. Surrendering himself to God, he receives from Him the return of infinite love—flooding every portion of his life till there is a new light upon the land and on every human face, and in his own heart a peace the world cannot give. This is the final humility, and it is the crown of intellect.

In this final act of liberation man is not alone. With him is the living companionship of Christ who knew, better than anyone else, the secret of the humble and the lonely insights of bitter revelation. During four years in college you will come on many great figures in the books of the world—Oedipus going home to Colonus in the twilight; Lear holding the dead Cordelia in his arms; Pasteur quietly triumphant in his laboratory; Faust brooding at midnight the mysteries of mortal satisfaction; the dying Hamlet, and the profound soul of Abraham Lincoln. These are our liberal education. But where will you find a man who, dying between two thieves, takes captive the world's imagination for two thousand years—the Son of God who says: 'Come unto me, all ye who are weary and are heavy laden. For I am meek and lowly of heart, and I will give you rest unto your souls." In Him is the end and the beginning of your liberal education; for the highest value you know is the value of a person. And where is there a person like Him? In Him is the beginning and the end of the mind's adventure. In Him the thoughts of God do become our thoughts; and His ways our ways. 'Higher than Him,' said Carlyle, 'human thought simply cannot go.'

To you who are with us for the first time let me finally welcome you with a symbol. When I was a boy, I went, one summer, on a camping trip to the Carter County Caves in Kentucky. One day, far back in the dark of one of the caves, I found myself crawling along on a ledge with a guide and a few companions. The light from our lanterns flashed back from stalactites and stalagmites upon the wall of the cave nearest us. Suddenly, turning a corner, I came upon one wall covered with the initials of campers who had preceded us. Among these names I discovered, to my complete surprise, the name of my father carved there many years before. I leave to your imagination the impression this made on a fourteen-year-old boy. And this is my symbol for you today. Your education, at the moment, is going forward in a cave. For the world just now does not wholly permit us to live in the full, clear light of the sun. Even so, you may proceed. This College will give you light and put a lantern in your hand. But your journey will hardly be complete unless, at some turning, you, too, may have the joy of discovering your Father's name.

# The Shining Enigma
## (1946)

About one hundred years ago, on a spring morning in Scotland, a young boy named Alexander Smith stood with a great throng in an open field some four miles northeast of Glasgow and watched the execution of two condemned men. Two poor Irish laborers who had come to Scotland to work on the new railroads had, in a fit of angry vengeance, struck a man down. They were being put to death on the very spot where the murder was committed. For weeks an impressionable boy, for whom his young world 'was like a die newly cut,' had followed every detail of the crime and the subsequent chase of the guilty men, as soldiers rushed here and there over the countryside. By night he tried to take upon himself the thoughts and feelings of the hunted and to apprehend the mystery of their desolate hearts. And now, in the May morning, he stood with the silent thousands before the scaffold with its black cross-beam and its two empty halters. He saw the blanched faces of the men who had so long occupied his dreams. The crowd grew stiff with fear and awe. Round the scaffold a wide space had been kept clear by the military; there the wheatfields 'were clothing themselves in the green of the young crop.' The swords of the dragoons flashed out to rigid attention; the cannon were all in position. Nothing stirred. 'Just then, out of the grassy space at the foot of the scaffold, in the dead silence audible to all, a lark rose from the side of its nest, and went singing upward' into the high blue sky. Some of you have seen larks rise, straight up, until they are lost to sight and become simply a vibration in the light, their song cascading downward in increasing power and glory the higher they rise. I know nothing on earth quite like it, and my memories are not as this boy's, standing in the fear-haunted field. Two men swift-sprung to their ghastly death, and the lark's flight not yet finished; from the fringe of a white May cloud his song still poured forth. Alexander Smith never forgot that moment. I confess I have not forgotten it either.

And this morning I want it to be a symbol of our thought. It is not easy to say the last thing a college has to say to those who have been with it for four years, especially for four years like these last four. One's comfort is, of course, to remember that the best things ever said by any college are never said at all—the great things that are beyond saying and either are or are not. Even so, for some weeks now I have tried to ask myself, "What is the *one* thing you would most like them to know? What is the best thing you think you know yourself? If education could leave a man with only one ultimate idea, what is that idea?' To let oneself in for this kind of meditation is, I assure you, no kindness to oneself. More than once, as I tried honestly to review my own time at college, my later stock of hopes and fears, doubts and assurances (and most of them are about what yours are, at least in kind), I found myself recalling old Archbishop Whately's comment on some who tried to think in his day: 'They aim at nothing, and they hit it.' Gradually, however, my confusion fell away and I knew clearly what I had to say and what I wanted to be Wooster's last word to you.

It is this: that, contrary to what is so often thought, the problem of good is a greater problem than the problem of evil. The fact that something in the world has been good should arouse in any careful thinker a greater perplexity than the fact that something has been bad. It should haunt him more and create for him far deeper questions. In a wonderful kind of way, it should fill the rest of his days with a divine mixture of annoyance and inspiration. It should keep his thinking straight and govern the practical choices of his career. The end of education, as I see it, is to know this: the shining enigma of life is not what is wrong with it but what is right with it. There is the bright puzzle to which all men were born to attend. That is why I wanted us to start this morning with that picture of sin and death a hundred years ago, and the terrifying lark rising from the green fields on a May morning.

The problem of evil has, of course, become classic. It comes home in myriad forms, and almost daily, both to the common man, who doesn't like it, and to the philosopher, who rather enjoys it because it at least gives him a lot to do. Part of what we see is our own failure and shortcomings—greed, envy, lust, indifference, pride, all the crocodiles that lie at the bottom of the human heart. We see also an evil that seems not of our own making—a world of war and earthquake, famine and pestilence, the mad and the maimed, a cosmic hallowe'en night full of witchery and fear. Blank walls of indifference surround a land of waste and accident, where there is both merited and unmerited suffering, when the blameless go down to ruin, where

> the good die first,
> And they whose hearts are dry as summer dust
> Burn to the socket.

The high stars wheeling overhead are careless of it all. Down the centuries one hears the ancient cry—the Greek chorus seeking the many shapes of mystery, Job calling from the depths of his despair, the voice of Macbeth startled by his own iniquity:

> Can such things be,
> And overcome us like a summer's cloud
> Without our special wonder?

Yet the problem of evil has an answer, and it gets one, too, from all sorts and conditions of men, whatever their different beliefs. To the Christian the possibility of evil is, for example, the price we pay for being persons. It is the cost of the risk God took in giving man his priceless gift of freedom, the dignity of choice, and a real share in the divine creative purpose. There are other Christian answers than this—not our concern this morning. The only danger in them all is that they are often much too smug and facile. God help us when we are so charmed by some celestial formula that death and accident and human suffering have lost their awful meaning for us. Before filth and slums and war and rotten politics and a secular society that gladly barters souls for dirty money, the first thing to feel is creative anger, the anger that gets things done. Then we can proceed to the nobler and loftier emotions, perhaps even to philosophy. Only by this road of practical resentment of evil, by opposing it in all its forms, does one really earn, perhaps, the right to know the wistful paradox of our personal freedom bought at so high a price. One thing we know, at least, this freedom cost us—the body of our Lord. Only when the day is far spent, when we have called black black and white white, when He has had the last ounce of our service and the best we have to give, can we truly stand at evening before the gulf that separates our partial knowledge from His wisdom, and say those words we have earned the right to say: 'Not our will, but Thine be done.'

The non-Christian has his logical answer too. To him evil is no enigma. If he be sufficiently saturnine, evil is the grim joke of some malignant deity or malevolent power. To a certain group of modern poets and thinkers the mind behind the world has not yet come to consciousness. It is, however, struggling along and things will be much better when the underprivileged deity learns enough to get promoted and acquires something of the pity and understanding of these spacious and lyrical souls who daily pray, one supposes, not to him, but for him. The answer I respect much more is that of any confirmed mechanist to whom evil is simply something that didn't work—a mechanical accident, or at best the chance bad dream of some slumbering electron. It is at

least an answer, a little invalidated simply because the thought of
any really confirmed mechanist is but the mere phase of a machine and therefore not really thought at all. There must be few
more melancholy embarrassments in this life than knowing you
cannot possibly have decided what you've decided. But here again,
come to think of it, the mechanist is saved. He doesn't know he
hasn't decided what he's decided; for actually he knows nothing
at all.

Evil then, for all its many forms, is not the chief enigma. The
shining enigma is the good. Here is the lark's flight in the scheme
of things, the excellence that begs to be explained. Here are loyalty and love and unstinting sacrifice; the wonder and beauty of
the world; the stunning plus sign life puts on so many of its
forms. To be sure, custom blinds us to these things; we get used
to most of them while we are children, so that we are too often
jaded by the time we are ready to think of them as parts of our
philosophy. The little baby is smothered with love and will have
to recover from his infancy. Maybe he will have to see the coun-
terweight of hate (we seemingly have to have a war) before he
can again inherit the earth and value love for what it is, the miracle of life, the crown of intellect, the intrinsic demand the human
spirit makes for immortality. But the good has a way of recovering itself.

Here is the plus sign of the good, a superb extra in life—far
beyond the routine demand of mere existence, beyond the need
of food, and sleep, and shelter, and physical desire. Try to explain
this plus sign in mechanistic terms and you have an embarrassment one cannot envy you. This is too much to ask of blind force
and matter without mind. It is too much to ask of mere chance
and accident. It is more than the slow round of evolution can
evoke unaided, without some prior hint of excellence that draws
it as the moon draws the sea.

> Dust as we are, the immortal spirit grows
> Like harmony in music.

Ask the mechanist to answer what one encounters in even four years of college—in great literature, art, and music; in the selfless devotion of the scientist to his inquiry; in social passion beyond calculation, in the whole heritage of what is human—and if the mechanist is a wise man he will have an immediate engagement out of town. For these are the great unnecessary things, the shining glories of the human spirit. Would you, for example, say that all that is decent and generous in you is only strategy and lynx-eyed cunning on your part? Or, perhaps, the result of some long process of social conditioning where some code of behavior has somehow been evolved? And even if you did say so, then explain this: 'Why *that* kind of conditioning?'

Personally, I have a better opinion of my fellow men. Were I to live three score and ten I would not have time enough to invent an explanation in mechanistic terms or in terms of some malevolent deity, of the miracles of love and mercy and understanding I have already received from the people I have known. There are the people (and we all have our separate lists of them) who should make us hold on to that great leading question we all try to dodge: what is the First Cause of these? Here are the facts, these people; the shining absurd *facts*. But why? A recent essayist living in Maine has said that after a light fall of snow on a winter morning he always feels 'humbled by the infinite ingenuity of the Lord who can make a red barn cast a blue shadow.' People can do more wonderfully than that, and it's a crime to miss them or fail to make them a major premise in our philosophy. One of the stunning insights of Shakespeare comes in *Othello*, where Iago, the brilliant villain, whose tricky mind seems to know everything and penetrate every human instinct, falls in the long run by sheer ignorance. One thing he did not know—that there were people like Desdemona, or a loyalty like that of Emilia, his own otherwise rather stupid wife. By missing the familiar excellence all about us we thus fail to possess the earth. And if we miss the sign of glory in our friends, how can we fully understand the greater people?

Actually we are so made that we love heroes and, when the natural supply of them is low, encourage even Mr. Barnum to contrive them for us. And if you think our hero-worship but a low form of mass vulgarity, explain then its shining opposite, the great American genius for loving the under-dog. If you think our language crude and full of bathos, explain why men respond to the great words in history—to the stark candor of Pericles addressing the bereaved of Athens, to Garibaldi saying to his men, 'Let those who wish to continue the war against the stranger come with me. I offer neither pay nor quarters nor provisions. I offer hunger, thirst, forced marches, battles, and death.' In the presence of such language we know that Emerson was right: 'From within, or from behind, a light shines through us upon things, and makes us aware that we are nothing, but the light is all.'

Let us not be afraid to praise the miracle of the good in us lest, in so doing, we seem to be over-complimenting man. There is a sharp cleavage in modern thought, between two rival camps—between the secular humanist who believes man can do all things through his own unaided effort and the theologian who, revolting from this very excess of humanism, stresses the total depravity of man whose only hope is God's grace and says, 'There is no health in us.' I confess to some sympathy with this latter group, largely because I am so weary of the former. A real sense of sin and of man's own inadequacy is a true step in the Christian experience. This is the door of realism and repentance through which the grace of God can come. But surely in man himself, if we look closely, must be some quiet intimation that he is worthy of divine attention, that he bears within himself at least the image of his Creator, that there are moments when he feels himself a partner, not merely in his own salvation, but in the whole redemptive work of God and man. And here, too, is an interesting paradox. The more a man does better his own practice and attains to a life of which he is not wholly ashamed, the more he knows the need of the divine mercy and senses the utter incompleteness of secular humanism. The more he lives by some moral law, the more he is aware that law itself is not man's final felicity. Above law and beyond morality, even while it includes it, is the completeness of Christian experience, where 'law, life, joy, impulse are one thing' and every instinct of the soul is in God's hands. To make a religion of humanism after one has known the larger scope of the Christian life is, if you'll let me say so in plain language, to commit the folly of the farmer who, finding the cat has entered his barn through a large hole, must needs cut a smaller hole for the kitten. But it is equally wrong to discount the godlike creative excellence in man—never more creative than in its longing after God's own grace.

Yesterday in this Chapel, honoring our dead from a second World War, we surely celebrated the enigma of goodness, as we heard the words of Ecclesiasticus: 'Let us now praise famous men'—even those who 'have no memorial.' 'Their bodies are buried in peace, but their name liveth forevermore.' The boy I thought most of yesterday was a former student of mine, a member of the class of 1936. When he was an undergraduate there were grave doubts expressed about the end to which he would come. It was believed in many quarters that he was a hopeless rebel, one who would surely end his days in Moscow. I had a great affection for this boy and trusted him completely. He talked rough at times, foolishly I often thought; but he had integrity if a man ever had. I especially liked him, I remember, for a very trivial reason. On examinations he answered only the questions that had been asked; he never answered the questions he was not asked. If you have ever taught, you know what a great thing this is. His hatred of war was deep; but he was finally in North Africa, in Italy. He won the Purple Heart, the Bronze Star, the Oak Leaf Cluster. He never got to Moscow as his critics had prophesied, for in the autumn of 1944 he died in France in the Vosges Mountains. Just a short time before, he wrote home: 'We have a long road to travel. Freedom's a hard bought thing.' I could believe in nothing and, believing in nothing, I would find Hitler no puzzle to me. But if I believed in nothing, I should have to give up before the enigma of Harold Spring. And he was but one of so many.

'And the earth was without form and void; and darkness was upon the face of the deep. . . . And God said, Let there be light: and there was light.' One of the important memories of my life is that of Toscanini's farewell concert as conductor of the New York Philharmonic a few years ago. That night his men were all eager to play over their heads as a final gift to their master; for many minutes before the concert began they were nervously picking and scraping away, tuning their instruments in a rasping orgy of sheer noise, exceeded only by the coughing and shuffling and excited talk of those who had come to share the biggest musical event of the year. The lights dimmed a little, and Toscanini himself appeared, the strange mixture of realism and other-worldliness that he always seemed to be. There was complete silence. Then a mind and spirit began to take charge of things, as what were once scattered fragments of discordant sound moved into pattern and order, resolved into a symphony and, finally, into the still more haunting appearing-and-disappearing structure of Wagner's *Siegfried Idyll*.

Only on one other similar occasion I can recall did I better learn how a musician frames, as Browning says, out of three sounds, 'not a fourth sound, but a star.' That was when I heard, as in a dream, another conductor lift a group of massed choirs and orchestra into the full singing and playing of the Christmas hymn, *Adeste Fideles*. 'Come, all ye faithful, joyful and triumphant. O come let us adore Him, Christ the Lord." Not just in His primal creation, but many times through many centuries, God, working often through men, has said, 'Let there be light,' and there was light—light, beauty, and order, and social passion, and excellence in all its forms. Perhaps God will speak again, through us, in our time. Someone in business, in politics, in international affairs will, maybe, speak for Him. If he does, he will say to us what Plato said many centuries ago to Democritus, hardly realizing the implication of what he said: The changeless elements of reality are not atoms; the changeless elements of reality are ideas.

Beyond the rising lark in the world of nature, beyond the rising of the human spirit in the jangled and disordered world of men, is still something higher than these. It is the cross of Him who said, 'If I be lifted up, I will draw all men unto me.' It is He who breaks all the enigmas for ever. In Him the shining puzzle of our partial good passes into the clear light of revelation—God made plain to us through the life and death and resurrection of His Son. Here is the heart of education. At least it is the heart of Wooster; of this hilltop that welcomes home this week-end, after years of war, its scattered sons and daughters.

# The Habit of the Soul
## (1948)

Two stories read to me when I was a child will likely remain
with me all my life. I had only one comment to make whenever
we reached the end of either: 'Let's have it all again.'

One of these stories was from Kipling's *Jungle Book*, the story
of Rikki-tikki-tavi, the remarkable mongoose who saved a whole
family from the cobras. He was superseded in my life only by
Dick, Tom, and Sam Rover and by the ubiquitous Tom Swift. I
liked the mongoose better than Tom Swift, because Tom
achieved his results through innumerable machines and gim-
micks, whereas Rikki-tikki-tavi did everything pretty much on
his own power. How many boys, one wonders, have read that
story? And how many battles he has helped to win for England,
as grown men who scarcely remembered him still carried some
fragment of his fine little courage in their hearts.

The other story was that of Jacob's dream. I had rigged up a
good many things in the backyard, but never anything as magnificent as that ladder between earth and heaven. The story still
has a strange power to move us, though the striking moment in it
now is, to me, a different one from what it was years ago. The
setting for the dream is, as it should be, charmingly indefinite.
Somewhere on the road from Beersheba to Haran, Jacob 'lighted
upon a certain place and tarried there all night because the sun

was set.' And he 'took the stones of that place, and put them for his pillows, and lay down in that place to sleep.' And in a dream he saw the ladder between the earth and heaven, with the angels ascending and descending. And the Lord spoke to him in the dream, saying, 'Behold, I am with thee, and keep thee in all places whither thou goest, and will bring thee again into this land: for I will not leave thee until I have done that which I have spoken to thee of.' The verse that then follows made no impression on me as a boy. But it does now: 'And Jacob awaked out of his sleep and said, Surely the Lord is in this place; and I knew it not.'

'Surely the Lord is in this place; and I knew it not.' Say it again and again, for there you have the symbol, not merely of spiritual blindness, but of what is our theme this morning—the tiny ideas, the thin and unworthy conception men too often have of Christianity itself. Most of us, from time to time, in one way or another, have conceived meanly of the faith we profess and of institutions such as colleges that are the outgrowth of this faith. We more than once could say with Jacob, 'Surely the Lord is in this place; and I knew it not.'

On this first Sunday morning of the new college year, we mark again the renewal of an effort that has been going on upon this hill for many years—the effort to combine a growth in learning with growth in the Christian faith. The world in general has more sympathy with that attempt than it had even a few years ago. It is a sympathy born of need and even of desperation. It is too dangerous to let the learned run amuck, if all they have is technical information. And I mean it as a compliment to your intelligence that I do not develop this point with any illustration whatever. You have already read and observed and shuddered at the world spectacle confronting your imagination. You have seen yourselves the essential truth in Justice Robert Jackson's striking summary: 'It is one of the paradoxes of our time that modern society needs to fear . . . only the educated man. The primitive peoples of the earth constitute no menace. The most serious crimes against civilization can be committed only by educated and technically competent people.' Dr. Jekyll has a companion now. The doctor's degree has also been conferred on Mr. Hyde—on those who would either freely use or be indifferent to the use of learning for brutish ends.

This is why educators are now willing to open their curricula to courses that only a short time ago they would have refused to honor at all. They are afraid now—afraid of Western man cut off from the culture that helped civilize him, of democracy cut off from the roots that fed its deepest faith in the dignity of human life and human brotherhood, of the modern mind tortured with its own inbreeding and absent from its noblest inquiry. They know that in this awful but still shining hour a new life must somehow be given to *people*. All this is good, and we should be glad to have part in the historic effort thus emphatically confirmed. It is good to see men waking from their secular dream and saying, 'Surely the Lord is in this place, and I knew it not.'

But what kind of awakening? To what view of the Lord? To what view of the Christian faith? To what notion of a college born of that faith?—a college that believes Christianity not just the object of a course of study to be grasped by the intellect alone, but a commitment of life, with laboratory requirements for mind and heart and soul, for meditation and for action. What could now pathetically spoil the Christian awakening in our modern world is a trivial conception of our religion.

Many still believe, including some Christians, that the faith we profess consists of three words: 'Thou shalt not.' Religion, they think, consists in what you *don't* do. They conceive of Divinity as one of Mr. Wells's English schoolboys would have conceived of it, as 'a limitless Being having the nature of a schoolmaster and making infinite rules.' God is the 'unrelenting eye' that, spying everywhere, never misses a thing. And many who are no longer schoolboys think of Christianity as a constricted, life-denying pietism, a touch of celestial frost that shrivels the bloom of the world. Likewise, a church college is often trivially conceived. It is judged in proportion to what does *not* happen within its gates —by its tidiness rather than its daring, by its regulations rather than its resolution, by what it deplores and opposes rather than by what it loves and nurtures.

To say this is not to deny for a moment the firm place of ethics in religion. Saying 'no' to many things is part of a Christian's business, though Christians will doubtless always differ as to the precise list of things to which 'no' should be said. Moreover, Christianity gives morality a sanction—the sanction that sin is something more than a mere lapse in prudence, that it is an offense against God and the abiding laws of life, against the love of God and a strange ingratitude toward His Son. Indeed, the whole failure of secular humanism and of nineteenth-century liberalism was their unrealistic optimism, their failure to see that 'no system of moral teaching will be effective divorced from moral power.' That moral power Christianity has furnished. And what is still more, it lights up morality, suggesting the deep joy that arises out of doing right. It offers creative renunciation. It persuades us to surrender this and turn our back on that, not just for the sake of obeying an edict, but that we may be free for some fullness of spirit, for stepping up the levels of life and life's appreciation. Christianity is the disciplined but inspired pursuit of higher significance. We give up one freedom to gain freedom of another kind. The fear of the Lord, Christianity has certainly said, is the beginning of wisdom. But Christianity has never said it was the end of wisdom.

The end of Christian wisdom seems to be something else. And we come to the heart of our thought in trying to see what it is. The striking difference between a Christian and another man is in this—the Christian's abiding sense of his relationship with God as revealed in Christ. This is the life-bestowing bond that seals his nature and gives him his distinction. Every part of every day he refers, as if by instinct, to something beyond himself to which he is none the less most graciously allied. He sees people in the light of God, and the smallest pleasures of mind and body are somehow emanations of God's bounty. No decision he makes seems wholly of his own making, and even his courage is not wholly out of his own heart. He has a sense of being a privileged partner in practical causes. He can wait and bide his time, out of some hint of things worth waiting for. Any talents he possesses are his simply as agent, and the best voice that speaks through his words and actions is a voice not his own. The sins and failures and perversities of his life are known for what they are—a reversal of his relation with his Lord; yet richly capable are even these of mercy and redirection.

This is the high unity of the Christian life where we see it at its best. Its secret is practical communion, and the life that flows from this communion. Even the parable of the ninety and nine comes thus to have a fuller meaning. The lost sheep is often cited as a symbol of the value Christianity places on the individual life. And this, of course, is true. But, looked at more closely, the main fact about the lost sheep was that it was out of relationship with its shepherd. The communion of the fold was broken. And so with men. The precious gift of God is this daily, eternal, common, magnificent bond of union—possible to us through the grace of God revealed to us in Jesus Christ.

One night, with a sense of discovery I shall never forget, I found in a sentence of John Henry Newman the kindly light that made all this very clear to me—clear as it had never been before. I hope these words may mean as much to you. Newman is discussing what faith means—faith, over which the tide of controversy has flowed back and forth across the years; faith, the word that frightens any young person because it suggests some tremendous act, some mysterious commitment of which, in all decent modesty, he may feel himself yet incapable. Then suddenly comes Newman's relieving word. 'Faith,' he says, 'is a habit of the soul.' Faith, in short, is keeping alive our relationship with God—the habit of living in perpetual reference to Him. It is not merely assenting to something that cannot be proved, but a sustained communication with the best we already know. The substance of things hoped for? Of course. But the rich ground of this very hope is in communion with the great Word on life already given us. Faith is attending to what we know.

Education, like most things, has its discipline, its necessary rules. They are the means to an end. But the final secret is not in them. The final secret, as Christ Himself said it was, is fullness of life in life's most significant relationship. Therefore, I believe with my whole heart that the real purpose of Christian education is to nurture in men and women this habit of the soul. The rest follows: 'The earth is the Lord's, and the fulness thereof, the world, and they that dwell therein.' This is the working faith one could wish for oneself, and for those one sees today in a place such as this.

Given this thesis, there are a few practical suggestions that immediately occur. First of these is the desire that this faith should be a reasonable faith. The habit of the soul enjoys support from the mind. Therefore, a church college must not and cannot be a conspiracy of silence about any fact of life that embarrasses religion. It must recognize these facts and try to deal with them as best it can. But it has a right to ask that no fact be studied in isolation, but rather in the full context of all we know and feel as men. It can wish that you have a tincture at least, of philosophy and that you know the great primary documents of the faith you either reject or receive, including I may add, and not naïvely, the Holy Bible. It can wish that you know some of the brilliant defenses made of the faith—not just by Crusaders and those who rode forth to fight some Holy War, but by those who have defended Christ upon the ramparts of the mind. The skeptics and atheists have always rejoiced in their spokesmen. We who believe need to renew our own esteem for, and certainly our knowledge of, those who have *thought* for us that we might have the ground of our faith preserved.

We can wish you also, even as we wish it ourselves, those exercises of devotion and attention that nourish the faith which is a habit of the soul. William James, you may recall, was once depressed by reading a story in which the heroine's charms were summed up in a phrase—she conveyed on all who saw her an impression of 'bottled lightning.' This was supposed to be a compliment. And Mr. Lowes, who comments on this, reminds us that one of our American ideas is still a man or woman who may be described as a 'human dynamo.' We need men of action to be sure. To work is to pray. The injunction to 'pray without ceasing' does not mean a knee perpetually bent or hands forever folded. Some of the noblest prayers to God have been the actions of the valiant in His service, standing squarely on their own two feet. But great action can be the fruit of meditation, and most of us need more quiet than we get.

This quiet I covet for you in the busy interplay of college life —quiet and direct communion. Sir William Osler, one of the great physicians of all time—and, incidentally, a very busy man— once wrote: 'I have always been impressed by the advice of St. Chrysostom: "Depart from the highway and transplant thyself in some enclosed ground, for it is hard for a tree which stands by the wayside to keep her fruit till it be ripe." ' Sir William, perhaps because he knew the habit of the body, also knew much about the habit of the soul.

We can hope, moreover, that a genuine central faith will confer some sense of proportion in our lives. Out of some standard of eternal worth we can then judge the conflicting bids for our attention—the plethora of empty stimuli, the whole elaborate quackery of the flimsy, the hectic, and the useless. All education is a growth in the power of discrimination, and this is no small gain. For one thing, it may save our wits and our nervous systems. It may help us escape from floundering in the sea of printed paper that daily tries to engulf our minds. It reminds us that the fashion of this world passes rapidly away, and that our true drift is toward what is abiding. It also helps us question the mass of things that need not be done at all.

But there is a crowning fruit of faith that is more than the inner peace it confers or the growth it fosters in discriminating judgment. The faith which is a habit of the soul lights up and transfigures with a new power of enjoyment and appreciation the world we live in. It brings together what should never have been divorced—the spiritual world and whatever in the material world deserves to endure. It makes education an exciting thing and puts research and inquiry in a worthy setting. It gives scope and range to intelligence and puts reason in its most exalted mood. It increases the homely joy of our daily association. It completes, in short, our liberal education.

We all know how a region—a town, a valley, a river, or a tract of mountain—can be transformed when a mind has touched it, when a poet or novelist, for example, evokes the genius of a place. We see Egdon Heath in new proportion and with heightened insight when we see it through the eyes of Thomas Hardy. Charles Lamb and Dickens have animated for more than a century the very face of London. Through Emily Brontë the moors of Yorkshire come to life; through Housman we see the west of England; and Ireland will borrow forever the afterglow of the Celtic Twilight. The English Lakes belonged to William Wordsworth, though no deed of ownership is registered in his name. With consecrated eyes he looked upon his native region, that exquisite land of water, hill, and sky—upon nature and on common life—so that a new power was given to men to see into the life of things. This was Wordsworth's gift to the modern era:

> for there was shed
> On spirits that had long been dead,
> Spirits dried up and closely furled,
> The freshness of the early world.
> (Matthew Arnold, "Memorial Verses: April, 1850")

One summer it was my great pleasure to go on a walking trip over the Lake Region of England. At every turn there was a light upon the land, a light conferred by him. Every bending of a road, the top of every rise of land, the peaks and the fells and valleys, the people who lived in towns or on the hillsides with their sheep brought its memory of him. So that one evening when we came to the old churchyard at Grasmere and found his grave there was little wonder at the plainness of the stone that marked his place. On all the other stones were lavish comments and extravagant inscriptions; on his this marking alone: 'William Wordsworth, 1770–1850.' That was all he needed, for everything around was his. And the companion of my journey said to me, 'What a pity it would be for a man to come this way and not see this land through him.'

What a pity it would be, here upon the hilltop you and I now know, were we not to see this land through Him to whom it belongs—through a faith in Him that is the habit of our soul.

Here we are privileged to complicate our minds as we will. Here is our chance to acquire, explore, interpret, and re-create. To serve Him we are not asked to give up this adventure of the mind, the enjoyment of our earthly good. We are asked, rather, to enhance this adventure and to see it through the eyes of faith. To do so, is to see it steadily and see it whole. And here, if we will it, a dream of Jacob can come true. A ladder can pass from heaven down to earth. Not in a dream, but in waking reality and fullness of life, we can say, 'Surely the Lord is in this place.'

This is the faith that is the habit of the soul. In this we are more than conquerors. Persuaded that nothing can separate us— neither height, nor depth, nor any other creature—from the love of God which is in Christ Jesus our Lord, we become inheritors of enduring life. It is not in far-off centuries or by distant tombs that one awaits the resurrection of the dead. That miracle is now —today, tonight, tomorrow—whenever man awakens with wonder to his true condition and comes upon that Easter morning that patiently waits for us at the bottom of our hearts. For even immortality may well turn out to be simply the eternal habit of the soul.

# The Transformed Journey
## (1949)

There is an abiding charm about Charles Lamb's famous dissertation on roast pig. No one would want to forget the delightful folly of the old Chinese villagers who, having once discovered the taste of crackling pork, deemed it wonderfully worthwhile to burn down houses—whole villages, if need be—to secure it. Four years of college, perhaps equally roundabout at times, are a lot of trouble, too. Who has not wondered if it were all worthwhile? Undergraduate days are full of annoying things—bills, professors, advice, rules, and delayed action. The weary weight of the unintelligible world presses on few people as it does on a sophomore. Yet, perhaps, all the trouble of college is worthwhile if it do no more than produce the unique felicity of baccalaureate morning.

Let us start with a symbol. It is from that familiar but inexhaustible book of symbols, *The Rubaiyat of Omar Khayyam*. Fitzgerald's lyrical rosary of desolation, a chant over the worldly hope men set their hearts upon, still speaks across the years, with its lament for desire that cannot be filled, and the rose of youth that withers in the moonlit garden. It sings with Oriental splendor to the passing moods of those who—often without needing poetic encouragement—think the one answer to all life's enigmas is 'a good, stiff drink,' and that

> Malt does more than Milton can
> To justify God's ways to man.

In the first edition of the poem—it was dropped from the one you and I best know—is the striking image:

> One Moment in Annihilation's Waste,
> One Moment, of the Well of Life to taste—
>   The Stars are setting and the Caravan
> Starts for the Dawn of Nothing—Oh, make haste!

I see there the symbol of a world well known in our own time: the stars of clarity and faith dropping in the dark sky; the camel-driver goading his steed to frenzied haste across the desert before him—for ourselves, the high-octane dash toward nothingness. Today, therefore, I want to talk about one of the striking aspects of our contemporary world: the benumbing and bewildering sense of pressure that bears down on men and women, the depressing whirl of change and flux, of meaningless activity and fear, without center or direction, the 'strange disease of modern life'

> With its sick hurry, its divided aims,
> Its heads o'ertaxed, its palsied hearts.

This is the desolate journey offered to modern men in so many ways. And over the wide desert many men are making it and wondering why. And as they haste along, pressed by they know not what, they feel themselves very old inside.

On this hectic journey there are many kinds of afflicted men. And each one of us, at various moments, bears some part in the affliction, for none of us is wholly a spectator. All the levels of life have their own special kinds of pressure. The ancient whips still crack above men's heads—the whips of lust, and greed, and power; of selfishness and false pride. There are the seekers of sensation, the tired, the bored, the vacant; the idle, the smatterers,

the doers of meaningless work. Towns and cities turn to the re-
volving iron cylinder set going by the Industrial Revolution.
There are the empty amusements that give no satisfaction, the
depressing mass of printed stuff, the low-grade politicians forever
yapping in other people's ears—triviality in triplicate. There is
the mighty galaxy of neon signs—red electric arrows stabbing
across the dark in front of the stores and the filling stations—the
endless goading of men into purchases they cannot afford to
make. Life presses on the little people who mean no harm to anyone but somehow get caught in the stream. Their modern symbol is the rather lovable Dagwood Bumstead, rushing from the
icebox to the bus. And, at the higher levels, the 'sensitive' people,
with capacity for thought, with pressures all the harder because
the pressures are often subtler and more imperfectly understood.
Haunted by the suspicion that there should be, if they could find
it, some secret to the spectacle that rushes before their eyes, they
know not what it is. They are struck at the heart with the rest-
lessness of being more than beasts, human beings unwilling to act
like animals in flight.

Our science and our literature are well aware of this condition
of modern men. Some observers feel there is no cure for it—that
our frenzy, internal and external, is the inevitable result of 'society in transition,' doubtless what Adam said to Eve as they left
the garden. Some resent it with anger and satire; some despair and
recommend retreat to Bali or some Pacific Island (the whole
trouble being that the islands, too, are in transition). Some sing of
our spiritual ferment in poetry or write of it in novels, deriving
what lyrical pleasure they can. And there is, of course, the new
kind of creature who botanizes over society and classifies what he
sees with a sick kind of scientific zeal. One remembers Emerson's
stopping a physician one day on the street to ask about another
physician who had been reported dying. 'I have not seen him today,' the first doctor answered—very joy sparkling in his eye—
but it is the most correct apoplexy I have ever seen, face and

hands livid, breathing sonorous, and all the symptoms perfect.'
And he rubbed his hands together with delight.

'Correct' or not, our present apoplectic spirits are not new. In-
tensified, to be sure, in the twentieth century, they are as old as
thoughtful time. Plato, Euripedes, Heraclitus, and Empedocles all
knew our modern questions. As more than one critic has noted,
Roman plumbing and Roman law, straight Roman roads and
walls could not conceal the twisted ennui of the Roman soul—the
weariness that chilled the Stoics and hurt the good Aurelius to his
heart:

> On that hard Pagan world disgust
> And secret loathing fell.
> Deep weariness and sated lust
> Made human life a hell.
>
> In his cool hall, with haggard eyes,
> The Roman noble lay;
> He drove abroad in furious guise,
> Along the Appian way.
>
> He made a feast, drank fierce and fast,
> And crown'd his hair with flowers—
> No easier nor no quicker pass's
> The impracticable hours.
>
> (Matthew Arnold, *Obermann Once More*)

All thoughtful time has sung the refrain of Omar Khayyam:

> The Stars are setting and the Caravan
> Starts for the Dawn of Nothing—Oh, make haste!

What has education done about the pressure and bewilderment
of modern life? Some say it has been merely aided and abetted. I
need hardly detail the charge. Education has, we are told, simply
spoiled the happiness and worth of too many men and women. It
has loaded their memories, dimmed their imagination, and
dwarfed their souls. It has—and the very charge is an interesting

paradox—either denatured man into a bundle of subconscious urges or made him a dry, bloodless creature of pure reason, divorced from emotion and will and faith. It offers him a political economy and a social science of stark materialism. It gives him dissonance for music, dirt for literature; and, for art, painting and sculpture that looks like something left over after an explosion. The science that was to have freed and exalted him is capable of our collective death, as little men play with big machines and forces that have outmatched their dwindling souls. The tree of knowledge, now in full harvest, bears its bitter fruit—the apples of discord, denial, and death. And what was once, even when it went wrong, only the leisurely danger of the aristocratic few, has become, with mass education, the corruption of the many. One hundred years ago exactly, a young man writing home from Switzerland noted in a letter the things that threatened and depressed him. At the head of his list is this entry: 'the height to which knowledge has come.' One hears the ancient voice out of Ecclesiastes: 'He that increaseth knowledge increaseth sorrow.' Thus runs the charge.

Is there no answer? Is there no education that delivers the human spirit from the flux of things, no education that can transform man's restless journey? Such education ought to be—and often is—the achievement of any Christian college giving a liberal education. In this aim, of course, no college fully succeeds. Yet, for all our failures, for all human resistance to instruction, men and women do leave here every June, with some secret that can transform their human journey and keep them young in mind and spirit till that journey's end.

Right education does this in many ways. It proposes a mind open to new truth. And with the receptive mind and its resulting freedom it suggests the counterpart—the responsibility for some commitment to a scale of adequate values. It teaches the critical spirit, the constructive critical spirit, of discarding what is less for what is more. It teaches us to beware of rumor and false report, and thereby saves us from many an internal spasm. It gives us the cool perspective of history, the companionship of ageless things with which we ourselves do not grow old. It gives us inner resources, the realization that we

> may not hope from outward forms to win
> The passion and the life, whose fountains are within.

The right education tells us homely things—that decency and honor give men a grace no art or sophistication can supply; that the one human trait that can open all doors of life and stop anything cold in its tracks is human character. Professor Duval has a favorite passage from Buddha: 'The odors of flowers, of sandalwood, and the fragrance of frankincense and jasmine travel with the wind but not against it; but the sweet odor of a good man travels with the wind and against it.' And right education teaches this, not just by rule and precept, but by giving us what someone has defined as the true end of education, 'the habitual vision of greatness.'

And true education teaches us to go to the depth of things and to decide only in the face of all the evidence. Liberal education—certainly Christian education—must face the evidence as the evidence is given. It cannot change the facts by pretending they do not exist or by diluting them. But it goes on to see—the words are from Wooster's own creed—'that the facts do not remain as scattered fragments but are considered in the light of all the rest we know as man.' It reminds us of the crucial human doctrine that man is the only judge the world of facts has, and that he himself must be studied in terms of his highest aspirations and insights.

True education helps us to detect the fallacy of those who ask us to deny our higher nature and its obligations. Mr. Freud, of course, has been unjustly blamed for a lot he never said, and some of his followers have exploited him. But do you know Lewis Mumford's devastating analysis of Freudianism and its modern result? 'In attempting to harmonize man's warring impulses, Freud,' he says, 'had no interest in bringing into existence a more life-enhancing super-ego [higher nature], the product of a maturer art, philosophy, and religion: his object was rather to lessen the weight of man's traditional super-ego, at least to cushion its pressure. For him art was a mere mechanism of escape, philosophy a rationalization, and religion an outright fraud.' Freud's followers drew the sinister conclusion 'that the needs of the id [i.e., the fundamental mass of life's urges and instincts] were more important than the curbs of the super-ego. . . . What does that mean but life without direction, without purpose . . . , life without any headwaters of energy, spilling aimlessly in every direction, undammed, uncanalized, therefore incapable of creating power or light? Once one rejects the creative role of the super-ego only two courses are open: the course I have just described, and the fascist's effort to create a positive super-ego out of the raw elements of the id: blood and carnage and booty and copulation, *as ideals*.' *

We have a sacred obligation, right education says, to follow all thoughts to their conclusion. For example, a college professor recently brought in to his class a book of two thousand pages. 'I want to impress on you in this way,' he said in effect, 'the sheer weight of time. If this book represents the history of the universe, then the total time of man as part of that is but the last page of the two thousand, and recorded history but the last three words of the last page.' A chill descends on us at that very notion. But think a moment, even if you accept this time-scheme. Those last three words—what words they are! In interest and grandeur and implication they are worth all the rest of the two thousand pages put together. In fact, there—in the last three words is the *new thing*, man—touched with contradiction, 'the glory, jest, and riddle of the world'—the only thing in the known universe that can create, pronounce a verdict, or even conceive of a universe, a being who, above all else, aspires—who transcends the world he has and reaches to something higher than the mere law of his own

* Lewis Mumford, *The Condition of Man* (New York: Harcourt, Brace, & Co., 1944), pp. 363, 365.

nature—'the body,' as Bergson says, 'now larger, calling for a bigger soul.'

And of these three last words there is one transcendent word—the Word made flesh, the Logos itself, the very Son of God. For there was another journey long ago, on a still and hallowed night. Here again the stars were setting and the caravan moved across the desert sands—not to the dawn of nothing, but to the dawn of supernal light. 'This was the night' to which, as one has said, 'the pagan world looked forward and all the later world looked back; this was the night that brought all time together.' Here, in a great event, the contradictions of our human life were resolved, caught up and transfigured in the miracle of love. The nature of both God and man stands clear in God's own Son, the *Redeemer*. Here the pressures cease, the whirling circle stops in what Dante long ago thought of, and a modern poet after him, as 'the still point of the turning world.'

In that divine life our own human journey is transfigured. From that day, across all space and time, stretches the open road that all men can tread who will—all sorts and conditions of men. Straight in the desert is prepared the highway of God. The valleys are exalted and the hills brought low; the crooked made straight, the rough places plain. Over His highway, on their transformed journey, go the young in heart forever.

# Values and Sanctions
## (1950)

Some of you recall the old fancy of how on the last morning of the world the sea will give up all its buried treasure. Merchant-traders, pirate ships, and men of war—all the proud galleons of time—will rise out of their dark depths. With sails crowding, their flags and banners flying, they will come thronging to the shore. Something of all this reminds me of baccalaureate morning. Not that the senior class has, in any way, been sunk. We think rather of the multitude of memories that rise to concentrate upon this hour. Memories of teachers, students, fathers, brothers, mothers, sisters. Memories of many kinds—of hopes and plans across the years, of strange interludes and anxieties, of obstacles overcome, of faith now justified. Only the dull of mind or the dead of heart can fail to catch the scope and meaning of such a morning, and its special quality as a kind of family affair.

It may be right, therefore, that what I have to say today happens to be born both out of memory and out of this family gathered here. Thirty-two years ago, at a time in my life when his sustaining voice was greatly needed, the grandfather of one member of this year's class spoke words I have never forgotten. Many times they have come back, with renewed and increased meaning. They are the germ, as I think you'll see later, of the one thing I most want to say now to his grandson and his grandson's classmates on the day before their graduation. Thus does the circle of time come round.

A sense of values, we are told, is the goal of education. All else is but instrumental and subservient. If we are to enjoy an existence worth having, if we are to exist, indeed, at all, we must be a discriminating race, conscious of the patterns and levels of life. There are differences in things. All information is not of equal worth. Colleges and universities have squirmed lately under the charge that they knew much about means but very little about ends, that they were spineless partners in the great national trust in 'big machines run by little men.' Many voices reminded them, with George Santayana, that 'never before have men known so many facts and been masters of so few principles.' So 'values' became the luminous word, and education now goes forth in its name.

This is as it should be. The natural sciences, social studies, philosophy, and the fine arts are joint partners in the quest. But the very search itself raises a new set of questions in thoughtful men. Where did the values come from? Who are we that are aware of them? Whence came these

> High instincts before which our mortal Nature
> Did tremble like a guilty Thing surprised.

These are questions that will not down. As the values become clear, the questions become clearer also.

When David Hume, for example, found himself responding to the high moments of great tragedy, he contrived an easy explanation of the whole effect. It is, he said, our response to eloquence and noble language. But, even if you thought this an adequate theory of tragic drama—and no one but David Hume has—you'd still have to face the deeper question, as more than one person has noted: Why are we so made that we do respond to eloquence and noble language?

There are even better questions. What gives these values authority? What makes the patterns of greatness come to life?

What magic do they possess that men will endure all hardship to serve them and even die for them? What happens when men find in their own nature the passions and instincts that war against such values? Clear sight of the mountain tops is not enough. The hard-pressed climber, weary and rebellious, and the night descending, wants to know if the high peaks are real, even in the dark. Have they some light shining behind them that commits us, imperfect climbers, to the climb forever? In short, what education must search for is not just values but sanctions for the values themselves—whatever gives them authority and power and attraction over the spirit of man, whatever makes them work and stick. What true learning really seeks is the highest sanction there is for the best in life.

The Christian faith believes it actually has this sanction—the power of making values real in the lives of imperfect men. It does this in two ways: by commandment and by attraction; by divine authority and by the miracle of love. The passage from Proverbs read this morning gives a hint of this double agency. Note it carefully: 'Let not mercy and truth forsake thee: bind them about thy neck; write them upon the table of thine heart.' There they both are—the law and love, the twofold sanction. Not the patterns of Byzantium, the city of static forms; but the living power of Jerusalem, the City of God.

Secularism, and most American education, of course, think Jerusalem is quite unnecessary. It is a ghost town in the new scheme of things. Secularism acknowledges but one capital, the city of Nature and Man. All there is and all we know is within the bounds of that walled town. Its streets are swept free of superstition. All the gods are in exile. We all know this city of Nature and Man, and we should be unfair not to give secularism, at its best, its just tribute. It was partly born, indeed, out of the stupid failures of religion itself. Wherever the church encouraged ignorance, bigotry, and hocus-pocus, secular idealism fought for freedom of thought and universal education. When the church closed its door to the needy, secularism fed men, healed them, opened clinics and hospitals, and cleaned up whole areas of social wrong. It gave the church some needed lessons on how to treat minority groups and cut through the wrappings of race prejudice. In doing all this, the secularist usually had the help of a deep religious heritage he refused to acknowledge. In the City of Man there is still a bank with a cross above its door where men borrow money from a window they swear is closed. If Jerusalem is a ghost town in the new world, the Holy Spirit has gone everywhere, and in all the ghost towns, even when unacknowledged, lives and moves and has effect, wherever good men hope, and dream, and act.

I would not weary you with any detailed account of the colossal failure of secularism in our time, both in our large affairs with nations and in our individual lives. Its debit side turns red. It fragmentizes and messes up the meaning of human life because it denies to life both its highest values and its highest sanctions. It gives us a brotherhood without brothers (since there is no common Father), a science that shuts its eyes to anything besides science and therefore stops even being scientific; it despises assumptions, and makes, as Dr. George Buttrick has said, its own sorry assumption that it makes no assumptions. It scorns religion but makes man himself a god. It covets the 'good life' but offers a relativism in morals that has no standards capable of moving the mass of men. Mr. Irving Babbitt used to enjoy quoting, as a symbol of moral relativism, those wonderful lines in *Punch* telling us how generous we ought to be with the Emperor Nero. After all, Nero was just a misguided, amiable youth who

> would have doubtless made his mark,
> Had he not, in a mad, mad boyish lark,
> Murdered his mother!

And secularism, scorning all that is divine, prides itself on being practical and down-to-earth. Actually, it is hopelessly unreal, and for one plain reason. It misses the two most notable things about people: their capacity to be low-down and their capacity to be great. It blinds itself to what the church calls sin and, even this side of sin, to the immense waywardness of the human heart, its vacillating character, its sheer laziness, if you will. Dr. Samuel Johnson, who could work himself like a horse when he had to, said that if he had 'no duties' and no sense of an immortal soul he would have spent his life 'in driving briskly in a post-chaise with a pretty woman.' We all know human failings—in ourselves—and though we may fall short of the great sinners, we have at least a sense of what they have been up to. Even the saints, in their honest moments, should repeat the old English song Hilaire Belloc liked so well:

> I am not a glutton
> But I do like pie.

But if we know our human capacity for sin and weakness, we know also our turn toward greatness—how our lives can rise like a star when the right voice calls them. We respond to the highest sanctions. Secularism worships experiment, but ignores the experimental evidence of how Christianity, as nothing else ever has been able to do, can literally make over the lives of men and women. 'These days,' says one of our best critics, 'everybody is himself, without reference to an idea—of God, for example.' Everybody is himself 'without reference to anything larger than himself; and so nobody is anybody.' Those are words to meditate. The only real defense against Communism, for example, is to breed in men's hearts the thing Karl Marx didn't know—that man lives not by bread alone (he needs that too, of course!) but by every word that proceeds from out the mouth of the spirit. Chancellor Hutchins reminds us that 'men, simply because they are men, are unlikely to find within themselves the power that can bring the good life and the good state to pass.' But let the divine trumpet sound along their blood in any land. Antigone, carrying in her heart the sense of eternal law, defies the edict of Creon; the glorious company of the Apostles goes forth, the noble army of the martyrs. And the earth bends beneath their footsteps.

Mark Twain, you will remember, in his *Innocents Abroad,* weeps over the graves of Adam and Eve as long-lost relations. But he also expresses some disappointment with them. How much better it might have been, he suggests, if the original garden had been turned over to some really competent people such as Martin Luther or Joan of Arc. 'At every critical pass in history,' William E. Hocking writes, 'you will find a man who is not taking his guidance from his fellows, nor his orders from social requirements; but who is rendering service which no man could demand of him, because his sense of the realities of the world leads him to demand it of himself. . . . For civilization can never outgrow, nor be greater than, the soul, which in its decision is always solitary, reaching out moment by moment into the realm of ultimate reality, and finding there, or failing to find, the sustaining resonance of a Will which is the meaning of the world.' Not just to the saints and the prophets either. To all the humbler people the idea of God 'peoples the lonely places' and gives enlargement of life. One feels this on any Sunday morning in any congregation. Plain men and women are exalted by their faith. 'It links them consciously'—as secularism never can—'with a larger order of things and sets their little lives amid the innumerable series of the years.'

Now the inquiring mind, the academic mind, stands easily in danger of one of the subtlest temptations of secularism. It is the danger of intellectual pride. The habit of forever learning, never coming to a knowledge of the truth, can seem to be rather distinguished. One respects honest doubt, of course; the true inquirer —the lonely voyager through the strange seas of thought. But one honors less the professional 'unbeliever' glorying in his unbelief. There are those who are 'so skeptical of dogma that they make skepticism itself a dogma.' I'll never forget a student—I liked him a lot—who said to me with white-hot fervor: 'I am *determined* always to keep an open mind!' Well, it is one thing to have an open mind, and another thing to have one that is forever open at both ends. Some who would despise emotion in religion allow themselves quite an emotional kick from sheer uncertainty and disillusion. Many a college student, if he must be caught in company with a book in his hand, would prefer it to be a copy of Voltaire or Nietzsche or Baudelaire than Butler's *Lives of the Saints; The Waste Land* of Mr. Eliot rather than his *Four Quartets.* And if it must be the Bible, let it be nothing more bracing and full of certitude than Ecclesiastes or selected parts of Job.

A few pale values, tentatively held, are deemed respectable; sanctions and blazing ubiquities are something that went out of fashion with Emerson. Professor Henry Steele Commager quotes these very significant words from a very good contemporary man of letters: 'The world is a kind of spiritual kindergarten where bewildered infants are trying to spell God with the wrong blocks,' and the important thing is simply the valiant, misguided effort in itself. That has a very familiar ring. Is that adolescent effort—when it is merely adolescent—less than the effort of those who think they have already seen some of God's real truth revealed in His Son? These are not afraid of reflective commitment. They go forth, not mincing as children, but as men with a divine warrant in their hands—bewildered, not by questions about God, but by the appalling weight of what opposes and rejects Him among men. Are *these* merely 'bewildered' children trying to spell God?—Jane Addams, Robert Speer, John Mott, William Booth, Frank Laubach, Stanton Lautenschlager? Are their names less worthy because of the truth they served? Surely few men must have had the intellectual's temptation more than Albert Schweitzer had it, with his questing intellect, his love of research, his capacious hand and brain. His life could have been one long precocious fugue in a minor key; but out of some divine sanction he struck the major chords of faith in a dark land. Must we assume that all the world must start from scratch forever? Is there no verified high history, by now is there no actual possession of the human soul? No permanence amid the flux of things? Against such miserable sterility the great heart of the world rebels.

This College asks no religious test of any graduate. We confer degrees tomorrow on a whole variety of minds and dispositions. We shall love the child of doubt as much as the child of faith. But we do hope this—that out of their study and experience those we send from this place will have some sense of what can happen when a human life feels the high sanction given to it by the Christian faith at its best. For this is part of the data of the world, a part of knowledge, something already discovered in the laboratory of life. It is a part of education, even for those who can't believe.

For religious faith does do things to men—great, plain things that he who runs may read. It gives meaning and power to even the fragments of existence. It saves from withering conceit him who learns early that any good thing he may manage to do is done not wholly out of his own strength—that a hand is behind our hands, a voice behind our voice, and that we borrow always, wherever we go, some life not our own. It ought to save us from fanaticism, too, and from the ugly excesses of intolerance and religious bigotry. For if one really believes that all men are the sons of God, he will never refuse to respect and weigh their views. He will feel, even when they differ from him, that they have something to tell him—that his freedom must not become self-righteous license to impose itself on other men. Do you remember Mark Twain's wonderful check on this score? 'In our country,' he says, 'we have those three unspeakably precious things: freedom of thought, freedom of speech, and the prudence never to practice either.'

We know, too, by now, how religion can make work a sacrament. Surely our country needs few things more than the sanction for this belief. Both capital and labor need it, and the sense of it in their hearts redeems them both, wherever it has been really felt. It is a very simple thing, this sense that all good work is an offering to God. Holding this belief, one need not, of course, be imposed on either by employer or employee. He can keep his eyes open and crack down when he has to, even in his own defense.

But, if this sanction were at the heart of contemporary life, we should have responsibility and freedom among men. Whatever they work at, they would work for Him in whose service alone there is perfect freedom.

One night Goethe went on an evening drive along the hills of Upper Weimar with his friend Eckermann. It was a thoughtful evening in which both men's lives rolled out in the perspective of the setting sun. When the night grew chilly and they went back home, Eckermann asked Goethe if he had not often thought how much the drudgery of his life—his practical, often menial work for the Weimar theater—had wasted his time from the creative writing that could so easily have always been his. 'Yes,' Goethe replied, 'I may have missed writing many a good thing, but when I reflect, I am not sorry. I have always regarded all I have done solely as symbolical.' *Whatsoever thy hand findeth to do*—so runs the homely doctrine, and the humblest person who does good work knows what it means. He knows also Him whose creative spirit moved upon the face of the waters at the foundation of the world. It is one of the great sacraments, this sacrament of consecrated effort. But a high sanction is needed for men to feel it.

Then at last, we see all about us the enduring power religion gives to men. I do not mean the power merely to bear one's human lot, to accept all living, 'both the dark and the bright.' I mean rather the power to give oneself to a noble enterprise, to take the high risks of life, to bring to some spiritual conclusion the resisting stuff of the actual world; to work and hope

> till Hope creates
> From its own wreck the thing it contemplates.

Such endurance has not been the monopoly of the religious. But no really religious person has lived who has not had it. For, if you believe in God, you believe in His order and His presence in it, and that His Son goes with those who know His love, even to the end of the world.

At Wooster we've tried to give you two things: an education and a faith, and some of it is bound to stick. Try believing that what was good here will be valid elsewhere—that the sanctions of your youth may be the sanctions of your old age. We've tried to tell you one amazing thing, something that only a place with Wooster's particular commitment can, with honesty, tell you: that life has, by virtue of divine love, the perpetual miracle of renewal. You can go from here tomorrow, whatever mistakes you have made here, as if you had just been born. And some day later, when you may feel some desperate need of it, you can be born again.

And so I come back at last to the words said to me so long ago by the grandfather of one of this class. He spoke of the great pagan philosophers and their remarkable scale of values—of Plato and Socrates, and the wistful Marcus Aurelius, the good Emperor, stretching out his hands toward some farther shore. And he told of how that pagan world seemed to know its lack of some higher sanction, as if its voice said, 'I see the golden isles; but oh for a firmer vessel and a surer word.'

Then he reminded me again of the sanction of Jesus Christ. One can reject His word—but, once hearing it, one cannot reject it perfectly. Wherever it is spoken and His name is named, the heart has a strange new knowledge. It has the eternal wager made to man—that he who will try to do His will shall somehow know of the doctrine. As William Temple, that brilliant, practical servant of God, said one night in London to his friends: 'We need One who shall give us a call greater than that which the nation has given—a call to dedicate everything to His service. . . . We may reject it if we like, as Jerusalem rejected, but it does not stay the coming of His kingdom. The very rejection was made the means by which He put forth His power, and the Cross of shame to which they nailed Him is the throne of His glory.'

The sanctions are with Him.

# The Remembering Eyes
## (1951)

One of the most delightful epitaphs in history marks the resting place of a great Irish scientist. It describes Robert Boyle as 'The Father of Chemistry and the Uncle of the Earl of Cork.' Into which of these two roles Robert Boyle put more of his Celtic fire, from which of them he drew the greater satisfaction, I do not know. But this happy mixture of learning and family ties, of brain and blood, somehow suggests the pleasant harmony of baccalaureate morning. I am not sure that we can call any member of the class of 1951 'the father of chemistry' or of history or mathematics. But one family tie is clear. To many of you, they are your sons and daughters. And tomorrow morning they will be sons and daughters of this place. The Dean and I have already signed the papers of adoption. Welcome, then, to a family reunion.

It isn't exactly the family reunion we might have liked. If I seem to pass by the uncertainties and anxieties of the present hour, it is not for lack of sympathy or concern. It is because there is, sharply clear against this dark background, something valid to say—something I am willing to risk as Wooster's last statement to its new sons and daughters.

To find it we must turn to Washington on the Sunday morning before Christmas, 1941. Pearl Harbor had been hit and we

were at war. Mr. Churchill had just come for conference and was
to speak next day to a joint session of the Congress. On this Sunday morning official Washington, Mr. Churchill, with the President, attended a church service. The preacher of the day was Dr.
ZeBarney Thorne Phillips. The scene I mention is described in
the remarkable memoir of him written by his daughter, Sallie
Phillips McClenahan. Near the close of his address that day Dr.
Phillips quoted the fine verses beginning:

> Guard the immortal fire.
> Honour the glorious line of the great dead.

One sees Mr. Churchill listening, his mind weary with two years
of war and the certainty of more, yet always capable of restoration at the sound of a strong idea.

> The lie may live an hour,
> The truth has living roots, and they
> strike deep.
> A moment's glory kills the rootless
> flower,
> While the true stem is gathering
> strength in sleep.
>
> Courage, O conquering soul!
> For all the boundless night that
> whelms thee now,
> Though suns and stars into oblivion
> roll,
> The gods abide and of their race art
> thou.

Yet, good as they are, these are not the words that strike me. It
was another line—one Mr. Churchill must have liked—that is the
sum of our thought this morning: *Truth has remembering eyes.*

This is a powerful statement, and, like most powerful state-
ments, it cuts a great many ways. The aspect of it I wish to stress
is this: whatever has stood well in the eyes of truth will stand; it
is not lost or forgotten. And anyone has a permanent possession

who has seen and known what the eyes of truth have remembered.

Education has been defined many times as what remains after you've forgotten all the facts you learned in college. There is a faint touch of rubbish in that. Some facts we don't dare forget. After the fashions have changed, after you have made a fool of yourself and known the worst that is written in your particular book, after the chisellers have chiselled you and the gyppers gypped you, after all the shots have been taken at your mind and heart and your faith—what do you have left, after you have lost everything they can take away? Whatever it is, that will be the best part of your education. It will be whatever you and truth have seen together with remembering eyes.

Truth remembers some very great things. And the comfort is that you can't miss some of these in four years of a liberal education. Our colleges and universities, the cynics say, have converted themselves 'as our drugstores have done, into something that corresponds only very loosely to their profession.' But a liberal arts college, whatever its other faults, has not done that. It is still, for most people, the best chance in America of avoiding what President Harold Dodds has called 'the worm's-eye view of life.' Because it looks higher than the worm looks, it sees some of the things truth has remembered and stored up for men and women as their permanent possessions.

What has truth remembered? You could make your own long list, and so could I. And I, who have the chance, will not. We can't tie up everything in a final sack and stamp Q.E.D. on it. Parents and colleges often have an urge to do this, but they can't. And even a baccalaureate address can't entirely put the world in final order.

For example, I think the eyes of truth very clearly remember the self-hood of individual men and women demonstrated many times through history. And I know of few things I could more covet for a college graduate than the belief in his own identity—

as something more than an animal, a chance chemical effect, the product of blind force, or the helpless sum of his own subconsciousness. But no baccalaureate hour can argue any college senior into a belief that he's a real person if he doesn't think he is. The proof of human personality, of individual worth and meaning, is a long effort in the world. The tyrannies of time and space and number, the mysteries of accident and evil, the stark zero life plants at the bottom of so many dead-end streets still war against man's faith in his own reality. This sea of faith, like so many others, is no longer full; modern man, bereft of his own identity, so often hears the waters running out—their

> melancholy, long, withdrawing roar
> Retreating, to the breath
> Of the night-wind, down the vast edges
>     drear
> And naked shingles of the world.

We'll give a diploma tomorrow, of course, to a graduate who can't prove he is alive—prove it to the philosophers, I mean, by logical demonstration. We'll do it out of a deep conviction that four years of liberal study give young people some great possessions—possessions beyond what they can logically demonstrate or sometimes even name. We believe that, if any graduate will stop to think of it in retrospect a moment, he will quickly see how a valid sense of selfhood does emerge in the very processes of liberal education, out of the very doing of the chores. Liberal study gives to the humblest person vocations and roles that belong to men and not to nonentities. You cannot be a zero and even make a stab at them. It creates persons, thinking and doing things that the eyes of truth have to remember in truth's own account of men. This silent knowledge of human worth and human validity, ennobling and sustaining, is the fine fruit of liberal education.

You cannot be a zero, for example, and be a seeker after truth itself. The very search makes you something. Reject the inquiring man, and all the rest is rejected—the hidden fact, the old fact that needs to be refurbished, logic itself, and the laws of nature, of which man alone is the discoverer. Mr. T. E. Jessop shows how any knowledge that devalues man is not knowledge; for 'the only creature that can prove anything cannot prove its own insignificance without depriving the proof of any proof value. Any radical depreciation of man involves an equally radical depreciation of the scientific thinking which supplies the supposed evidence.' It is hard to beat that. And any honest, inquiring student knows in his heart that this is so. Surely the eyes of truth remember those who seek her with diligence, even though the quest itself falls short.

If truth honors the search for fact, it surely honors the search for values—the quest which raises fact-hunting to the art of criticism. Zero cannot hunt values, let alone live by them and cherish them. And liberal education does well—it makes persons of us —when it encourages the growth of our critical faculty. By criticism I do not mean mere griping and literary blood-letting, in which the American college student is not likely to be excelled by any student in the world. True criticism always carries its own restraint. There is an old Chinese proverb: 'Do not remove a fly from your friend's forehead with a hatchet.' Criticism does not mean doing that. It means detecting the lie and the half-truth. You remember how old Josh Billings used to say that it wasn't ignorance that did him in; rather it was the things he 'knowed that wasn't so.'

Criticism means learning the best in order to have a standard, the preference of higher things to lower things. It means learning that truth and goodness do not consist in bigness. Bernard De Voto praises New England for its immunity against this particular plague. It is impossible, he says, to imagine Concord tattooing itself with signs calling itself 'Villa Superba; the Sunlight City of Happy Kiddies and Cheap Labor.' Criticism means resisting also the notion that the good life consists in things. Gilbert Seldes, in

his fine satire, 'The Man Who Went to Pieces Entirely,' ironically tells of the disintegration of one James Mortimer who had
to drop out of contemporary life because he was unfitted, by
some quaint logic, to believe all the advertising that he read. He
gave up shaving because the problem of big and little beads of
lather simply confused him. He gave up radio because he grew
tired of 'the cryptic signals of police sergeants calling to their
mates.' And when he vanished out of life entirely, he left a note
scribbled on the margin of an advertisement: 'Cf. Spinoza. We
think things good because we desire them, we do not desire them
because we think them good.' Mr. Seldes says, 'I think he simpli-
fies Spinoza a little, but I see what he was driving at.' Perhaps the
eyes of truth will remember him.

Liberal education tries to make persons of us not just by its invitation to the quest for knowledge and the quest for values. It
gives a third gift—the actual possession of beauty and excellence.
A zero cannot possess such excellence, but the human spirit can.
Its stature rises with its own beholding. During four years on a
college campus a man or woman must be dull, indeed, to miss the
accent of excellence in all its variety of forms. The world is
charred with this divine grandeur:

> It will flame out, like shining from
>     shook foil.
> It gathers to a greatness—

And the beholding of this is part of selfhood, authentic, undeni-
able.

And it is wrong to think of such beauty and excellence as mere
decoration. It is deeply needed as the leaven in a democracy, for
the saving of democracy's own soul. Do you remember Mr. Walter Lippmann's analysis of Jane Addams, the great social worker?
In what, he asks, did her greatness consist? 'It was the quality
within her which made it possible for her to descend into the pits
of squalor and meanness and cruelty and evil, and yet never lose,

in fact always to hold clearly, the distinctions that are precious to a maturely civilized being. She had compassion without condescension. She had pity without retreat into vulgarity. She had infinite sympathy for common things, without forgetfulness of those that are uncommon. That, I think, is why those who have known her say that she was not only good but great.'

Liberal education suggests something beyond the search for fact and values, something beyond excellence and beauty. It commands the love of good men and good causes. Dostoievsky long ago saw that negation disappears before the active love of one's neighbor. 'This,' he says, 'has been tried. This is certain.' And he does not mean the phony humanitarianism such as the doctor in *The Brothers Karamazov* expresses: 'I love humanity, but I wonder at myself. The more I love humanity in general, the less I love man in particular.' And the sound love of good causes—reflective commitment to things worth fighting for—is the privilege of genuine persons. The scholar's objectivity can refine his judgment and temper his excesses, but it should not deny him a man's privilege of loving and hating the things he should love and hate, the privilege of staking all he has on the loyalties that matter.

Dr. Oliver Carmichael reminds us, for example, that pre-war Germany had the largest percentage of Ph.D.s of any country in the world. 'It developed science and the scientific method with a thoroughness not found elsewhere. And yet it was this same country that permitted a Dachau, a Buchenwald, a regime of unbelievable atrocities. The leaders of Germany, despite their intellectual training, did not have the character and integrity to withstand Hitler. Their courage and convictions yielded before his fanaticism.' The uncommitted intellect surrendered to the first committed brute that came along. The eyes of truth will not remember the irresponsibles. It cancels them with the other zeros of life.

The highest truth of the self, however, is not its selfhood. The researcher, the critic, the lover of beauty and excellence, the fighter for good causes has only an inadequate humanism if the world stops with him—if beyond him there is nothing else. The something else, of course, is the great secret of religion. Hundreds of men and women have possessed it, and truth has seen across the centuries the amazing exhibit of the free bondsman of God. As Dr. Ganse Little put it, the Christian view of life holds that 'entirely aside from what I want to do, there is something God wants me to do—there is a truth about what my life is meant to be: that, entirely aside from what I think, there is objective truth—what God thinks.'

This is not food for babes, or easy doctrine for willful, unaided man. It would be hard going as philosophy or theology, for it demands the surrender of self. But it is made possible for us in the life of Jesus Christ. 'The simplification of anything is always sensational.' And, in this high sense, Jesus Christ is sensational beyond measure. In Him what was philosophy in Eastern Asia became 'life, biography, and drama.' The eyes of justice were kept blindfolded that there might be impartial law; but the eyes of truth are open to everything, to see beyond the law the ultimate mercy of God. They saw the Son of God, who wrote no books and invented no system. He wrote only once, as far as we know —in the sand. But He left us His sublime, spontaneous life and conversation. 'It was not for any pompous proclamation,' says G. K. Chesterton; 'it was not for any elaborate output of printed volumes; it was for a few splendid and idle words that the Cross was set up on Calvary, and the earth gaped, and the sun was darkened at noonday.' And the eyes of truth saw and remembered.

And since then, over the centuries and across the world, men have been persuaded that something does last, something that remains when everything has been taken away that can be taken away—that 'neither death, nor life, nor things present, nor things to come, nor height, nor depth, nor any other creature shall be able to separate us from the love of God which is in Jesus Christ our Lord.' For known unto God are all His works from the beginning of the world.

The faith some of us have in Wooster does not rest, I hope, on flimsy sentiment, a moonlit night, or ivy-covered walls. It rests on something of what I have tried to suggest this morning—that there have been real things here, things that truth will remember. We believe you will remember them—wherever your road now leads or how far away you go.

# Lodging-Houses and Homes
## (1952)

Some hours of life mean a great deal, and this is one of them—
one of the few things left in the world that you would prefer not
to see by television. We wish it were a somewhat different kind
of baccalaureate morning. We wish there were a clearer, less in-
terrupted road ahead for some of your sons. And if we say no
more about that, set our silence down to a deep faith in them.
For, if anyone thinks that our present graduates are being handed
a beaten-up world gone dead on our hands, let him remember
that the class of 1952 has not been without a certain considerable
vitality. You may recall how Oscar Wilde one day in Paris
gloomily remarked to his friend Turner, 'I have had a dreadful
dream. I dreamt that I was dining with the dead.' Whereupon
Turner answered, 'Well, my dear Oscar, I'm sure you were the
life of the party.'

Our theme comes from a remark of Dr. George Buttrick in his
book, *Faith and Education*. 'Modern man has tried the suspense
of believing nothing, and because suspense is soon unbearable, he
has ended by believing almost anything. . . . That is, modern
man has no home, but only a succession of cheap lodging-houses.'
There is our symbol. And before we suggest what it can mean,
let us put round it two or three qualifications. Surely Mr. But-

trick would not—and I certainly will not—be ungrateful for the good lodging-houses of the world. Time has taught me this: anybody who runs a good one will have his other sins forgiven. And even a mediocre lodging-house seems now a little like a haven, in these days of vast, uprooted people, 'the armies of the homeless and unfed.' Moreover, if you look at it one way, a lodging-house might indeed be the symbol of the on-traveling mind, rigorous in pursuit of truth, preferring an honest stopping place, however temporary, to some factitious home he really has not earned.

But the cheap lodging-house, contrasted with a home, as we intend it, means what is transient, unworthy, unsatisfying. It is the fourth- or fifth-rate situation we have chosen over the first-rate. It is the compromise, the shoddy place we have accepted for our body, mind, or spirit that, down in our hearts, we know won't do. It is the opposite of what is real and excellent and fair, the abiding places of significance, where, beyond the pressures, the flux, the meaningless activity, we know a center and direction, and sense how

> satisfaction is a lowly
> thing, how pure a thing is joy.

Mr. Eliot has something of this in mind when he projects the squalor and ordinariness of so much of our common life in one sharp but sympathetic image of the coming of morning in a great city:

> One thinks of all the hands
> That are raising dingy shades
> In a thousand furnished rooms.

What are some of the cheap lodging-houses of the modern spirit? Where have we accepted inadequate and unsatisfying abode? I have no wish to detail all our present discontents. All of us read and see and hear, and we know ourselves. And, if we don't know our troubles already, both political parties will be telling us during the next five long and windy months. The mark of 1952 is fairly clear. The London *Times*, in the superb mid-century edition of its *Literary Supplement*, notes this main fact about us—that the 'air of elegant scepticism which was worn so gracefully during the 1920's and the early 1930's has vanished.' In its place is 'an extreme malaise'—a deep anxiety, 'an unusual thirst for belief—whether the object of belief be religious, philosophical, political, or simply social.' This desire for some better attachment and loyalty affects not just the 'intellectuals' but the 'whole run of people.' 'Dissatisfaction,' says the *Times*, is the 'residuary emotion of the age.' People want to belong to something better than the things they belong to now. They are sick of cheap lodging-houses. They look round them for homes.

Actually, a man's house is no longer what it used to be, in its stature and solitary importance, even when it was the center of a great estate. Once it was perhaps a place, a landmark of distinction—something it took hours or days to drive up to. Now it is a spot or blur that it takes less than a second to zoom over. But our modern lodging-houses are not just homes that have lost something of their former dignity. They are subtler than that. The things that badly house our spirits are the familiar tenements and slums of the mind and soul: ignorance, the half-ideas, the thin information, prejudice and hatreds that corrode us, the wrong kind of ambition, the vast effort we make to please all the wrong people, our indifference to causes and fights we ought to be in, our preoccupation with mediocrity in its hundred forms. In our hearts we are ashamed of all this, and our shining gadgets do not ease our shame. We are tired, too, of all the 'guff'—the formulae that have lost their reason—such twaddle, for example, that it is 'sweet to die for one's country.' Necessary to die, maybe. Noble to die, perhaps. But never sweet. It was a Roman who said it was. The Greeks never said it. As one fine critic has pointed out, the Greeks had a great tragic drama. They would not soften life with sentimental rot. They knew the sharp difference between good and evil, life and death. They never sopped their minds with any of the 'vital lies.'

Our modern Ulysses wanders, not over the 'wine-dark seas,' but from one dry house to another—too often no adventurer, but the aimless, drifting spectator. He wants comfort, but he does not want to earn it. He wants repose without, as Hawthorne says, 're-linquishing evil.' He would like to leave the lodging-house, but lacks the will to check out. Or else he begins to find the lodging-house itself quite comfortable and even necessary to him. He fondles what was past, dwelling in self-pity or nostalgia on all the world did to him or he to the world. Or else he has an unsatisfied, pitiable hunger for something better than he has, a deep urge to belong, a yearning for self-realization—for identity.

A recent English critic cites, in this connection, our high rating of the novels of Thomas Wolfe, our willingness to overlook his obvious faults as a writer because he expresses how deep our hunger for self-realization really is. This critic reminds us of the lonely boy in *Look Homeward, Angel*—of the boy's desire to prove his own self in a world of others. The boy felt that 'no matter what leper's taint he might carry on his flesh, there was in him a health that was greater than they could ever know.' . . . He would register in hotels as ' "Robert Herrick," "John Donne," "George Peele," "William Blake," and "John Milton." . . . Once he registered at a hotel in a small Piedmont town as "Ben Jonson." The clerk spun the book critically.

' "Isn't there an *h* in that name?" he said.

' "No," said Eugene. "That's another branch of the family. I have an uncle, Samuel, who spells his name that way." '

One hears, across the centuries, the old refrain of Saint Augustine: 'Our heart is restless till it rests in'—well, rests in something, at any rate.

And, often, when men do move out on some spiritual quest, they turn, not to some homeland of strong belief, but into some form of 'religiosity' which is a pale substitute for religion—into poetry, and fine feelings, and noble sentiment, into a secular idealism that lives off the pale afterglow of our father's faith. Mr. Winston Churchill quotes another critic's keen judgment on Bernard Shaw: 'All his life Shaw has suffered under a handicap, which is that he is shy of using the name of God, yet cannot find any proper substitute.' And when a man does turn to church, too often he finds, not a home for his spirit, but just a new kind of lodging-house; not a community of forgiven sinners transformed into new life, but rather a 'community of the saved,' who, in Reinhold Niebuhr's acid phrase, 'have brought the meaning of life to merely another premature conclusion.'

All this is the 'religiosity' that even in death is creating, especially in California, the gaudy final resting-places called 'Memorial Parks'—with 'the largest wrought-iron gates in the world,' 'dreamy, nebulous, dissolving' music, all 'bird-song and evergreen, plashing water and tesselated stone,' with strains of Carrie Jacobs Bond and Sigmund Romberg 'warbled from loud-speakers in the ivy,' together with general, vague advice about tuning in with the Infinite. 'No intimation,' continues my late friend, Dixon Wecter, to whose satire I am indebted, 'of the real meaning of death, no symbols of Christian suffering, and but scant suggestion of Christian hope.' And Mr. Wecter wonders if these fashions are the prelude to some end of an older, cleaner America, 'the church in the midland village, the city cathedral, the New England spire above the town green, and also the quiet cemeteries where lie eight or nine generations.' Death has its cheap lodging-houses, even when the bill is high.

Little wonder that from the narrow concept of life has come a narrow view of what our real home in the world is—the failure of our international imagination, our dull notion that money alone, unaccompanied by brains and heart and understanding, can buy the love of our neighbors, or that our real home is the whole world, inconvenient though this may be. Little wonder the key-word of modern life is 'fear'—so much so that when Alan Paton some months ago wrote his description of South Africa and its dark, involved strife, it seemed like a larger comment on mankind:

> Cry, the beloved country, these things are not yet at an end. The sun pours down on the earth, on the lovely land that man cannot enjoy. He knows only the fear of his heart. . . . Cry, the beloved country, for the unborn child that is the inheritor of our fear. Let him not love the earth too deeply. Let him not laugh too gladly when the water runs through his fingers, nor stand too silent when the setting sun makes red the veld with fire. Let him not be too moved when the birds of his land are singing, nor give too much of his heart to a mountain or a valley. For fear will rob him of all if he gives too much.

And anxious men, tired of a miserable temporariness and all it breeds about the heart—without center, direction, or home—saw in the lodging-house of South Africa all the stark and fearful lodging-houses of the world.

If higher education has one supreme thing to do, it is this: to show man the roads that lead to the true homes of his own spirit, to give direction and center to his life. People fuss a great deal about the objectives of education, and argue about them and about them. I remember a winter evening in a hotel in Atlantic City, where all day I had listened to teachers debating the goals of their profession, and without much result. I noticed with sudden delight that across the hall from us another convention was going on. It was the Mosquito Exterminators of New Jersey. Their objective was perfectly clear; they were united by one deadly aim. But education has never been that single-minded, and probably should not be. It tries, at its best, however, to go beyond the lodging-houses. And it does this in two rather different ways. It tries to provide a general pattern and perspective, which is one kind of home; and the mastery of one field, which is another kind. And over all of it should brood the high task of a college as Gilbert Highet defined it: 'to cast such a light on a man's youth as will illuminate him through his life, and yet to keep the light unblurred.'

The way of illumination, the lamps that light men home, are not new. They are the learning of critical distinctions between what is less and what is more, something of the precision and the spaciousness of natural science, the creative power of great art and music and literature, a sense of the humane past that frees from the 'chronic childishness' of living always in the present, an instinct for creative work and pioneering, the high friction and rub of heart-felt chores that keep our lives from aimless spinning like a jacked-up wheel in high gear. These, and a conscience for what needs doing in the world to stir the blood. Some enlightened love of other people, then some friends and a faith. These are the things that lead us home.

A faith is the center of it all. And education is a poor thing if it does not make the chance of having a faith one of the live options of an undergraduate career. The homing pathway out of the cheap lodging-houses of life is God's love revealed in His Son.

Two blocks stand across that pathway, and they are curiously very different. One of them is the block of intellectual pride, the 'syllogistic dryness' that withers the noble faculty of reason and makes it too small to catch the play and interplay of life itself. The other trap is the very opposite of reason—a belief that there is no reason, at least none of any avail; the belief that we are the helpless victims of the subconscious and the dark and bestial things within us. There is even a kind of enchantment in this view. I sometimes think that in our country, not patriotism, but the glands will turn out to be the last refuge of a scoundrel. What a travesty is our depth psychology when it fails to go deep enough, when, below all the raw root stuff it can so easily find it fails to find the deeper golden ore that runs in human beings. This is why, perhaps, the theologians who, rightly revolting

against the cocky secular humanism of a cocky rationalism, do
well to watch their step in stressing man's corrupt nature in their
very proper emphasis on sin. Sin, yes; corruption, yes. But, below
the sin and corruption, some shining buried vein of something
that at least God thought well enough of to let His Son die for in
the hugger-mugger of the world. Beneath the 'explosive stuff' in
us that reason is so often helpless to control, there is a deeper
hint of our true nature and destiny—'something in us,' Rufus
Jones used to say, 'that did not originate in the world of matter,
in the time-space order. Someday . . . the deeps below the deeps
will be found, and there in the darkness and quiet we shall come
upon impressive and convincing proof of Him, who dwells both
in the darkness and in the light.' 'The eternal God is our home,'
said the Old Testament book we read this morning. Then the
centuries passed by and there was a new way of saying it. There
was a great event in history. It is still going on. For, as Canon
Leeson says, it is in 'the face of Jesus Christ that the glory of God
shines.'

You remember, toward the end of *Paradise Lost,* Milton's fine
account of our first homelessness. Adam and Eve are leaving the
paradise they were not able to possess. A great company of
cherubim arise, much as the evening mist rises out of a river.
Michael, the archangel, takes Adam and Eve to the eastern gate
and down the cliff to a flat plain. Looking back, they see a ring of
fiery faces above the gate, and a flaming sword above it, standing
straight up, barring their return forever. They move out across
the plain, toward all the lodging-houses they and their children
will inhabit through all the generations.

But they carry a strange secret in their hearts. Michael himself
had given it to them only a few minutes before—that the redeeming love of God was yet to be made known in a wonderful
unique way; that Man might yet possess a paradise within himself, happier far than any he had lost. The kind of paradise it
would be was not too clear. It would be something like home.

But it would also be something like the Kingdom of God, for that, too, is within us. 'This having learnt,' Michael said,

> 'thou has attained the sum
> Of wisdom; hope no higher, though all the stars
> Thou knewest by name, and . . .
> All secrets of the deep.'

> The World was all before them, where to choose
> Their place of rest, and Providence their guide:
> They hand in hand with wandering steps and slow
> Through Eden took their solitary way.

Any college, while you are in it, will seem more like a lodging-house than a home. But the roots of home, of all the homes a man may ever know, are there. It is a matter of record, at any rate, that men and women all over the world look back here and find a center and direction, a spur and comfort for their journeying. Many of them have known sickness and disappointment; a few have taken death and martyrdom for the sake of something they learned here that they thought was so. They are a proud company, and we are proud to have you join them. I think they will like you, as you, still young in heart, travel the homing highways of the world.

# The Touch of Greatness
## (1953)

During the last ten years we have heard many pronouncements, many theories of higher learning. Some of these have been good and will wear for a long time. Others are already vanity. The remains of them lie profusely around us, like the ruins of broken castles in the Irish moonlight. Out of the welter, good and bad, one statement about education seems most to have caught men's minds. It keeps cropping up in meetings, in formal papers, in personal talk—wherever men and committees meet. It is Alfred North Whitehead's remark that education should afford 'the habitual vision of greatness.' Well, that's vague enough, and very exalted. It is not too useful, one might say, in deciding practical questions. But it is, at any rate, the remark that has stuck. It has made more sense to more people I know than any other thing said about education in recent years. It makes sense because it reflects what is deep in the human spirit. It matches the longing in men's minds and souls. And so this is the claim I would make for higher learning—it lends to human beings, even the most ordinary human beings, the touch of greatness.

The Renaissance was once defined as the movement that put humanity 'in the way of great things.' And I prefer to use the word 'greatness' rather than 'excellence' because it has as tall a connotation and a grander range. It has little, of course, to do with size. It has everything to do with quality and magnanimity and nobility. The word be what it will, this solid claim can be made for a college course: it puts men in the way of great things. In spite of all the faults of students and teachers, nobody can easily live for four years in a liberal arts college and escape the touch of greatness. He may well be touched by a lot else, of course; but this other touch will be there, too. It may walk hand in hand with the dull, the sterile, and the picayune. It will come even to him who does not especially deserve it—to him who has wasted yards of his precious time. But mediocrity and insincerity cannot subdue it. Against the contagion of such excellence 'the sensual and the dark revel in vain.' The very breath of it is in the air. For, as Emerson saw long ago, one learns in life, not just by working but by being worked on. There are silent and even un-merited acquisitions of taste that make possible 'the deeper de-lights.' For those who have really striven toward understanding, the reward is even more. 'To have known the best and to have known it *for* the best,' is, as Professor Mackail pointed out, suc-cess in life. At any rate, we suggest the likelihood that the abiding part of education will be some touch of greatness. And as we give this assurance, let us think of greatness for a moment—our suspi-cion of it, the ways it comes to us in liberal study; the need we have for greatness, and how even the humblest of us has the prac-tical chance of sharing in it.

We are, of course, suspicious of greatness. The very word is over-worked and misused. Last summer in Chicago at the two po-litical conventions a 'g-r-e-a-t American' bloomed on every microphone. In that same city, years ago, one remembers, a cer-tain man of letters was followed to his grave by what the papers described as 'forty of Chicago's major poets.' Even at the high moment of the Coronation one unfortunately recalls the impish ob-servation that the peerage is the best thing in fiction that the En-glish have ever done. Little wonder we come to feel that great-ness is something too good to be true very often.

We also come to feel that even true greatness has nothing to do with us. One of the growing dangers of the world is the sense that the individual life counts for so very little—that the common man turns helplessly in the iron cylinder of contemporary fate, while the great ride far on the mountain tops, determining mighty events, planning the expeditions and the wars, and riding down now and then, Valkyrie-like, only to pick up the wounded and the dead. Tomorrow morning, please observe, our commencement address by Norman Cousins is entitled 'What Can One Man Do?' The very question is part of our modern temper. Surely we all know how much of the ordinary and the humdrum is our regular and necessary portion. Education and life are loaded with homely chores. This is what I heard in our house the other morning: 'Mt. Everest is climbed; the Queen is crowned. Now to wash the dishes and send out the laundry.' Perhaps you heard something like it in your house, too.

And yet—for all the chores, for all our disclaimer that greatness has anything to do with us—we turn to it as flowers turn to light. We feel starved when there is a dearth of it in our nation and in the world. We have a singular loneliness without it, and rally to it as to the sound of a trumpet. And any higher education that does not covet the touch of it will die on the vine or become 'a vast whirl of machinery in the void.'

Certainly any liberal education worth the name makes the forms of greatness real. It puts us in the way of them and lets them work on us. It opens the life of logic and reason and, beyond that, a world of the imagination, which is 'Reason in her most exalted mood.' It teaches fine care for detail. It suggests the great curiosities—those questions that go through life with us, that sift and vivify experience, that lend point to reading and travel, that set up rich networks of association, that fire the mind to nobler effort, that keep the inquiring heart and spirit unwearied and young forever. It shows us, by many examples, the scientist's love of cool inquiry, the clean reaches of impersonal thought divorced from self-interest and benumbing passion. It reveals the quiet greatness of the poised and modulated mind, of that quality Charles Morgan found in the best of Max Beerbohm's prose—'the illusion of sunlit conversation when it is near evening and the great heat is gone from the day.'

Again, in art and music and literature, in the taller documents of politics and history, we see greatness. And we see it, not in bloodless abstraction, but in warm and living embodiment—not in musical sounds, but in music; not poetics, but poetry; not principles of design, but paintings and statues. Every nuance of our common life has had some memorable statement, when a mind has touched it to splendor. How the great words ring in our ears: Wordsworth with his keen notice that

> The swan on still St. Mary's lake
> Floats double, swan and shadow.

Or, on another level, King Henry, in the dark of the early morning before Agincourt, heartening his little company of soldiers:

> From this day to the ending of the world,
> But we in it shall be remembered;
> We few, we happy few, we band of brothers.

Or Lincoln in his own dark hour:

> The occasion is piled high with difficulty, and we must rise—
> with the occasion. . . . We shall nobly save, or meanly lose,
> the last best hope of earth.

Or the still older voices:

> If I take the wings of the morning, and dwell in
>     the uttermost parts of the sea;
> Even there shall thy hand lead me, and thy right
>     hand shall hold me.

These and so many others—the living forms of greatness that have touched all of us. They have constituted so much of the best

of our education. They come both out of the present and out of
the past—not so much, in Lowell's phrase, 'out of tradition, but
out of the original and eternal life out of which all tradition takes
its rise.'

The touch of greatness comes also out of biography. How
much of the education that really sticks is our encounter with
great natures and great character. Sir Richard Livingstone reminds us of the letter Cicero wrote to his son who was starting
out for Athens: 'You are going to visit men who are supremely
men.' Education should say that, too. For at every turn we read
or hear of those who show us, by example, the power of truth
and goodness and nobility in human life. We see how the world
is 'upheld by the veracity of good men.' In them we learn the
difference between light and shadow. We see devotion and patience and the faith that there are, as someone said, 'certain eternal achievements that make even happiness look like trash.'

In 1897 a young man in the bicycle business in Dayton, Ohio,
suggested to his brother that they go into the business of building
automobiles. 'No,' replied his brother, 'to try to build one that
would be any account, you'd be tackling the impossible. Why, it
would be easier to build a flying-machine!' Four years later, according to his biographer, Wilbur Wright came home after a
series of discouraging experiments with a glider, saying that 'not
within a thousand years would man ever fly.' But he and his
brother persevered in their unrewarding work. Then, in two
short years, the miracle at Kitty Hawk. We celebrate this December the fiftieth anniversary of that event. The very account
of it affords the touch of greatness in human example.

I am glad that we are free here to include in a liberal education
the high issues of philosophy and religion. How this came home
to me, as it must have to some of you, the other evening as we
watched the pictures of the Coronation. There was the Abbey
with its bright candles, its fabulous jewels, the flashing splendor
of crowns and coronets, the ermine and the golden vestments.
Then suddenly the Archbishop of Canterbury and the Moderator

of the Church of Scotland stepped forward to present a Bible to the Queen, saying as they did so: Here 'is the most valuable thing that this world affords. Here is wisdom; this is the royal law; these are the lively Oracles of God.' Pitiable the higher learning that is not free to say to students what men have said to the kings and queens at their crowning, 'Here, above your own majesty, is the highest touch of greatness.'

And if we believe that liberal learning can and does afford this touch of greatness, let us not forget our utter need of it. We need it ourselves, as a personal possession—to set for us the lines of character, the nice balances of freedom and responsibility. It can give us possession of the spirit destiny cannot destroy, and weave through the broken fabric of our lives the thread of great things. It can help us to distinguish between the ripples and waves, to know that short-range prejudice is not eternal principle. It can teach us to wait and bide out time; to look foolish, if need be, for some ultimate end; to follow a quiet course of imperturbable thought and action. 'We must interest ourselves,' President Hadley used to say to his Yale colleagues, 'we must interest ourselves in the things that are really large . . . to give us a sense of the size of things as they come before us.'

If you and I need this sense, how much society as a whole needs it—how much our nation needs it, and the world needs it— in our search for freedom and order, in our search for quality in our common life. Greatness of one's country does not lie in size, or possessions, or power, but in desiring, as Viscount Cecil remarked, to be 'in the van of intellectual and moral progress.' In his remarkably interesting book, *The Big Change*, Frederick Lewis Allen describes the American people as those to whom things have come pretty well to hand. In 1950, in a land of 59 million civilian laborers there are perhaps 59,300,000 car drivers. 'Never before in human history, perhaps,' Mr. Allen says, a little wryly, 'had any such proportion of the nationals of any land known the lifting of the spirit that the free exercise of power can bring.' We have thirty-eight magazines with a circulation of more than a million apiece. We have complete communication— day and night. We know by heart the sound of Toscanini and of Uncle Miltie Berle. But need we despair, out of some snobbery and academic niceness, that, in this mechanical paradise, where doors swing open at the touch of light, minds may not be opened in the same way? But, you will say, excellence is not common and abundant. Of course not. It never was. But it does have power, and the effect of it can be widely spread. Walt Whitman was being only half fanciful when he described 'the arrival of the Muse, a migrant from ancient Greece to the New World' :

> By the thud of machinery and shrill steam-whistle undismayed,
> Bluff'd not a bit by drain-pipe, gasometers, artificial fertilizers;
> Smiling and pleas'd with palpable intent to stay,
> She's here, install'd amid the kitchen-ware!

Beyond even our added forms of culture, both men and nations come at last to the subtle task of transcending their own selves. This problem of sublimation is at the very heart of our lives. It is not the low problem of escape—by being amused or busy or drunk. It is the higher problem of being lifted out of oneself and transformed by the love of things that are higher than we are. God help the man or nation who thinks it can be done some other way. You can be clever and able and armed to the teeth with the tricks of your trade. But the tight little world of you and chromium will never satisfy your longing soul. The longing soul demands the touch of greatness.

Yes, you will say. Education can be full of these things. But are they intended for us ordinary folks? So we circle back to the old misgiving with which we began: 'Is all this really for me?' I believe it is, with all my heart. The day I stop believing it I shall get into some other business. I believe this not because there is greatness and a human instinct for it. My confidence, my whole faith as a teacher, rests on a deeper ground—that is, on the ground of the Christian faith itself.

In this faith there is utter realism—the frank recognition that there are no perfect men, who might have a corner on greatness and hold it for their own. There is the recognition that all of us, you and I included, are a mixed lot and very often not so much. But, alongside this recognition, is the equally realistic faith, proved time and again, that life can be touched to finer issues, that sin can be forgiven, that life can start up again even after it has fallen flat on its face. And this conviction reposes, not on the mere wishing of ordinary man or on the fine dreams of some philosopher. It rests on example, on the shining Son of God Himself, who showed us what perfection was and in such a way that we did not find it strange. Beauty, and truth, and love arrived with Him and knocked at the door of even the lowliest heart: 'I am come that ye might have life.' 'Behold, I make all things new.' And men heard His voice, on the Damascus road and on the countless highways of the world ever since. 'At midday, O king, I saw in the way a light from heaven, above the brightness of the sun, shining round about me and them which journeyed with me. . . . I heard a voice speaking unto me. . . . Rise, and stand upon thy feet. . . . Whereupon, O king Agrippa, I was not disobedient unto the heavenly vision.'

The Christian faith we hold does not say, however, that you and I and the rest of us will ever be great ourselves. It cares almost nothing about that. But it does say we can really know what greatness is—that we can love it and care for it, and hang on to it, and fight for it; that, loving it, and caring for it, we can be transformed by it. The ultimate measure of us will not be how bright or gifted or lucky we were. The measure will be how much we opened our minds and souls to the light around us; how much we loved light and tried to work in its name. This is the last thing a college ought to say to anybody. And we say it now, in the name of Him who is Himself the light and shines more and more, world without end, even unto the perfect day.

# The Gift of Fire
## (1954)

It is over a hundred years since Mark Twain grew up in the little 'white town' of Hannibal, by the side of the Mississippi. He was all boy—and then some. His mother, looking back from her later and much quieter years, remarked that he had given her much more uneasiness than had any of her other children. Whereupon Mark Twain asked his mother whether it was because she had been afraid he wouldn't live. 'No,' she replied, her eyes dancing, 'I was afraid you would.' Our first greeting to you who come with us to this baccalaureate hour is the official assurance that your sons and daughters do deserve to live. This has been solemly decided by the faculty and the board of trustees. It has the finality of Malachi. We have watched students tempered by the weather, independent study, various other kinds of free enterprise pursued both night and day, and by the ingenuity of trying not to let their parents down tax-wise by earning, in this land of initiative and opportunity, more than six hundred dollars in a given year. Tomorrow we shall present them to you and rejoice with you in their sudden splendor of sheepskin, tassel, and rented gown. 'Your sons and daughters—A.B.!' After which the old world can go on, as someone said, to teach them, as it teaches all of us, the rest of the alphabet.

A college wants its last word to those who have been with it four years to be, if possible, something straight out of its head and heart. It is not easy to decide what that word is. And my choice this morning was fixed in the homeliest of ways. In a very good book of epitaphs, *Stories on Stone* by Charles L. Wallis, I happened to see this strange memorial off a gravestone in Girard, Pennsylvania:

> In memory of
> Ellen Shannon
> Aged 26 Years
> Who was fatally burned
> March 21st 1870
> by the explosion of a lamp
> filled with 'R. E. Danforth's
> Non Explosive
> Burning Fluid'

That much brief notice—with its plain historical turn, its un-elaborated tragedy, its lapidary smile of revenge nicely taken, its clear warning to future purchasers of Mr. Danforth's fluid! Round that bizarre record of the past gathered the thoughts of this morning—questions, and symbols, and beliefs about life, and colleges, and the human spirit; about the world we know and the world we hope for; the dreams of the old and the visions of the young. Unmistakably I knew that what I wanted to say to those who were leaving us was this: if Wooster has given anything to you, I hope that among its gifts is the gift of fire.

There are, unfortunately, two widely held conceptions about colleges that imply education has nothing to do with fire. The first of these conceptions is less worthy than the second. It is the polite notion that the aim of learning is merely to put a cool, sleek finish on a young man or woman and assist him to a secure and respectable place in the world, with a minimum of strain and certainly no explosions. If the fountain of knowledge runs at all,

it runs something like Mr. Danforth's fluid. Nothing is set on fire
—and an explosion would be as out of taste as an ink blot on a
copy of Lord Chesterfield's letters to his son.

To say this is not to depreciate the practical rewards of a college. A liberal education can be and usually is a vocational asset.
If it happens to include a care for good health, good manners, a
sensible management of time and talent and money, and an enjoyment of some of the finer graces of life, there is surely nothing
very wrong with that. A man does not necessarily prove his
learning by being an eccentric, a boor, a wild-eyed zealot, or by
resembling in his dress what Heywood Broun's close and affec-
tionate friends used to say of him—'nothing so much as an
unmade bed.' To acquire a measure of calm good sense, to know
almost automatically something of the rules and amenities of living, has this too frequently unrecognized spiritual and important
result—it frees one for attending to really significant matters. But
a college can recognize all this without making tidiness and re-
spectability the highest good of mankind. If it points only toward
cool contentment without the ardor that redeems and honors all
true living, then a college deserves to be defined as one man in a
recent survey defined it. 'A college,' he said, 'is anything with ivy
on it.'

The second misconception is nobler. It is likewise incomplete.
It assumes all learning must be cold. Reason, the chill and dispassionate goddess, dwells by the lorn ice-packed streams in the thin
mountain air. To be wise is to be diffident and even bloodless.
The owl, for all his feathers, must be cold. Anything warm or
vibrant, anything below the timber line, is suspect. Van Wyck
Brooks records President Eliot's wry comment on Harvard:
'Things seem to be going fairly well, now that a spirit of pessi-
mism prevails in all departments.' The trouble, of course, with
the conception of university as a mental frigidaire is that it gives
no true account of the best minds, the best observation, the best
reasoning, or the best attainment. This is no time, certainly, to
undervalue the cool pursuit of anything—when many a head

seems clearly heated beyond its abilities and the love of truth seems but 'the faintest of human passions.' Yet value objectivity, and accuracy, and straight logic, and all the icy virtues as one may, we somehow know that the highest things in the world—in science as in other areas—are not all born in cold blood. So much of our highest excellence is the history of the gift of fire.

It is really three gifts, or, rather, three kinds of fire. And the first gift is the fire that consumes. Its purifying flame, born of unfolding excellence and standards and impassioned values, runs through our ordinary lives like a transforming agent. We commonly think of four years in college as years of acquisition and fulfillment, and this is so. But let us remember also how much of any good education, how much of any spiritual growth we know in life, is the history of renunciation, the history of what is consumed, the history of the gods that arrive when the half-gods go. Then it is that a man knows within himself something that is like the clearing of the stubbled fields in the early spring. The rubbish of our accumulated days goes up in smoke before the touch of great things. We have often so much to burn away—our petty jealousies and hatreds, our conformity to what is not worth conforming to, the 'deep slumber of our decided opinions,' our lazy contentment with inadequate ideas and inadequate information, our surrender to all the hogwash that daily tries to engulf our eyes and ears. We all know it well when into our lives comes the white fire of deliverance, lit often in high places and in great souls centuries ago—fires born in agony and exultation, in the 'good, the great, the wise in all the ages.' Whenever fire is struck from the finer flint of the world, the humblest of us is aware.

And nothing consumed in it can be better spared than those two dark enemies of living—our pride and our fear. What is one of the surest marks of a truly educated man? Is it that he knows enough to know how wrong he can often be, that he has brains and experience and gratitude enough to know that a man does nothing of himself, because all that is blest is borrowed? We have no margin for false pride. Mr. Charles Kettering, of all men, has lived a life of sheer creation. Like Tristram Shandy's father, he has intercepted many a thought that Heaven must surely have intended for another man. But when I asked him the other afternoon what word, if any, he might care to send to a little group of scientists and others meeting in Cambridge, England, two weeks from now, his answer came like a shot: 'Tell them that science has one chief problem—our gigantic overestimation of what we are supposed to know.'

Like pride, fear is a giant in the world just now. Understandably so. Our dangers are real, and our stake in the world is high. But, as Professor Henry Steele Commager reminds us, two centuries ago Benjamin Franklin, enlightened realist that he was, wrote the all-time words on this hot subject: 'They that can give up essential liberty to obtain a little temporary safety deserve neither liberty nor safety.' When will we learn that? What consuming fire can take away from us, not our right and proper caution, but our mean, ignoble fear?

And the fire that consumes teaches us something more, which is perhaps the best it teaches us. It shows us what cannot be consumed, the golden things that remain when the alloy and the dross are gone. This is the business of colleges: to suggest what is indestructible, what abides after 'the fashions of the world pass rapidly away.' The enduring things that, like the heart of Joan, will not burn in the marketplace of Rouen; like the soaring eternal song of redeeming love in the wonderful close of Wagner's *Götterdämmerung*, rising in transcendent violins beyond Brünnehilde's funeral pyre, and burning Valhalla, and the fire-swept twilight of the gods.

> The splendours of the firmament of time
> May be eclipsed, but are extinguished not;
> Like stars to their appointed height they climb. . . .
>
> The sun comes forth, and many reptiles spawn;
> He sets, and each ephemeral insect then

Is gathered into death without a dawn,
And the immortal stars awake again.

(Percy Bysshe Shelley, *Adonais*)

The second gift is very different. It is the fire that sustains and inspires. Unlike the consuming fire, it is full of friendly warmth and is wholly creative. An undergraduate comes to know and feel it in many a quiet ordinary moment as well as in the moments that will be memorable, the moments that will have authority over all the rest of his days. He will find it in the disciplines of a library or a laboratory or a competitive sport. He learns the slow fires of the long patience, the enduring heart that man needs for any sustained endeavor. He sees the multitudinous homely chores, not as drudgery, but as the 'great ordinary means' to perhaps a great, extraordinary end. The young scientist thinks of Pasteur, plugging away at the crystals of racemic acid, without the slightest notion that what he was doing might have practical value. As George Hale has said, suddenly Pasteur saw that fermentation was not, as it had been regarded, purely chemical process. He 'showed it to be due to the presence of hosts of bacteria, which eagerly devoured one class of crystals and ignored the others. This was the beginning of that great study of putrefaction changes, and of the part played by bacteria in disease, which was to make the world Pasteur's debtor.' Men like that live by the still warmth of the mind that keeps them going till the inspired blaze of the crowning moment comes. Do you remember how Edison conducted 28,000 experiments on a new type of storage battery, making a careful record of each successive failure? A reporter, we are told, asked him 'if he did not consider the work as wasted effort. "Wasted effort?" Edison exclaimed. "What do you mean, wasted effort? I now know 28,000 things that won't work."'

This warming and inspiring fire is the fine contagion of universities. In the social sciences, in the fine arts and the humanities, in philosophy and religion, men find themselves susceptible to immediate causes that become the loyalties of a lifetime, and to per-

spectives and insights that give a large frame of being to all their
days. They learn to hate what should be hated and to love what
should be loved. They see that being merely bright and clever and
correct simply will not do. They outgrow what Mr. V. S.
Pritchett called the 'middle-class gentility' that preserves men
'from the great disgusts.' They learn even from those they imperfectly understand, because they respect their quality. Mr. Julian
Hawthorne tells us that of all the old Lyceum lecturers at Concord the best liked was Emerson. Even when he was over the
heads of his hearers, they wanted him. 'As we were leaving the
hall one evening I overheard Prescott, the grocer, say to Jonas
Hastings, the shoemaker, "Did you get that about the Oversoul?"
. . . Jonas shook his head: "No use wondering what he means;
we know he's giving us the best there is." '

Sometimes the warmth that inspires is not anything that takes
command of a life or lifts the whole spirit of a man to high endeavor. Quite often it is a very simple thing—the swift and small
delights that come with art, and music, and reading. To my grave
I shall remember the pleasant ardor for the mind that arises from
such things as Dylan Thomas's line, 'The force that through the
green fuse drives the flower,' or from one small phrase in the
score of Brahms's *Requiem*, or from Carlyle's brief comment on
the celebrated Goddess of Reason the people of Paris honored in
the French Revolution. Carlyle describes the enormous fuss made
over her, and then comes one simple added remark that Reason
had one difficulty. 'Her teeth,' he says, 'were defective.' These
are the small, quick flames that light our way along the world.
And, when the pressures are on and we feel the weight of the
immediate hour, suddenly we are warmed and sustained by the
glimpse of some perspective, some image out of time. I remember
the great delight the late Desmond MacCarthy used to take in
that passage from Anatole France: 'The bright stars, so full of life
and animation, covering in the May night the campagna of Rome,
of Umbria, and Tuscany. I have seen them from of old, on the

Appian Way, round the tomb of Caecilia Metalla, where they have been dancing for two thousand years.'

I like to think that part of the warmth that sustains and inspires arises very often in a real teacher's concept of a student. Sir Ernest Barker, the English historian, says that he idealizes his students 'because I wanted to serve them, and because I could serve them better if I saw them not in the cold light of what they actually were, but in the warmer and brighter light of what they might become.' Nobody could accuse Alfred North Whitehead of softness of intellect. Anybody who encountered him knew that his mind was magnificent, 'terrible as an army with banners.' But he was all fire and warm light as a teacher at Cambridge and Harvard. I think one of his conversations, recorded by Mr. Lucien Price, gives us the clue: 'There are ideas,' Mr. Whitehead remarked, 'which have lain in their tombs for centuries, then rising again, have revolutionized society. Some boy who is more than merely bright gets hold of an idea which has long been supposed to be dead, and it comes to life in his hands. For when a young man is all in a glow over the discovery of a great idea, it is not so much the particular idea he has discovered that is important, as it is his glow over it.' Thank God for that kind of warmth in a great teacher. It cannot be sold or bought. Little wonder when Mr. Whitehead was asked if he saw 'any bulwark' against atomic destruction of civilization, he made this quick answer: 'Only the appearance of half a dozen eminent men.' And he, alas, died some six years ago.

The third gift of fire needs little comment. It is the fire that illumines, the fire that draws near to light. Above all else, this is what we would like to have. The fire that consumes and the fire that warms? Yes, to be sure. But beyond everything else we would like to know what is true. This is the clear point of understanding we seek from birth till death—the light at the heart of the fire.

For centuries now, men have thought of Prometheus. He is the hero of the long legend of fire. According to the old myth, he stole the bright gift from Heaven for the sake of men. Civilization was to be advanced by it. In the *Prometheus Bound* of Aeschylus the drama is hard to interpret, because it is part of a trilogy otherwise lost. Prometheus, bound to his rock in the high Caucasus, fed upon by the vultures, is the enigma of the clash of human reason and either aspiration or self-will against the eternal power. In the later poets he becomes, of course, the daring friend of man, the suffering servant and deliverer.

Were we to write that tragedy now, it seems to me that for the moment it would be a drama of humiliation to us all. The Titan who won the gift of fire and we for whom he won it would be huddled in shelters underground, lest the blessed flame he wrought from the chariot of the sun be now rained down on all our heads. The drama would have a new atomic title—perhaps *Prometheus Burrowing*. The chorus of the play is already written, it seems to me, by the poet of our time who tells us that we shall be consumed now either by 'fire or fire'—either by the hot and seering flame of our own invention or by the fire of reason and imagination and divine love that devours the other fire and transfigures it to the glory of God and man. And so, in such a time as this, we want one thing: the truth. In desperation now we try to see the light at the heart of the fire.

When men have thought of Prometheus they have thought also of another, and linked his name with the name of Jesus the Christ. Both are the suffering servants of mankind. And, like Prometheus, our Lord brought with Him, wherever he touched men's lives, the gifts of fire—the fire that consumes and purifies, and the fire that warms and inspires. All history is full of His glory on these scores. But He brought also, as Prometheus did not, the fire that illumines. So, very simply, we say there is a third gift, the fire that is entirely light. We say there was once One who was not just another great man in history. He was the Incarnate God. And the truth of Him is mercy and peace, loving-kindness and commitment to a life that in itself is a triumph over death. This is the most important thing any college has to say to anyone. Take Him into your life and your whole journey will be hedged with fire. The promise is as old as Pentecost: 'I will pour out my spirit upon you.' For Jesus of Nazareth, a man approved of God, is the suffering servant, the risen Lord, the King of Glory, the Light of the World. And 'this promise is unto you and to your children.'

# The Primary Sources
## (1955)

Our theme this morning bears a quiet title, derived from a very
old academic phrase, 'the primary sources.' By it we mean the
first-hand things, the authentic ground of facts and ideas, the
original wells and springs out of which all the rest either is drawn
or flows. The true scholar will always be found regarding them
and near to them. Against them he tests all assumption, all second-
hand report, all vague generalization. They are the point of re-
pair, the enduring nourishment of the eye and the mind. And one
of the main ends of a liberal education is to learn respect for them
and to keep returning to them all through the years.

The primary sources have far more than merely academic significance. They can inform and transform every phase of our existence. For they do a kind of double duty. They can keep us
straight and near the truth of things. And, beyond doing that,
they can supply the deep centers of power and inspiration out of
which the best of our life can arise. Both these services are crucial, the first being the prerequisite of the second. First of all, we
have to be saved from the avalanche of rumor and guff, the
welter of lies and half-truths that roll in upon us. In every matter
of our common life there is at least one primary fact, one thought
of greatest worth that has the veracity, the amplitude, the power.
The business of a man is to find what this is. No second-hand,

roundabout approach to it, no pale derivative of it, no looking at it in the tin mirror of somebody's fancy will ever compensate the lack of the shining original itself. It was perhaps said unkindly of one of our English philosophers that 'his idea of a tragedy was a deduction killed by a fact.' The quest for truth requires a basic humility—the willingness to see what your eyes really see, even when the sight hurts your wishes and your pride.

Regard for the primary sources makes one forever the enemy of preconceptions, of manipulated data, raw opinion, and guesswork—of all the sleek short cuts to wisdom in ten easy lessons. To say this is not to depreciate the legitimate works of synthesis, the broad views and conclusions that can themselves become primary sources for a new age. Nor is it to despise the guides and charts and surveys that lead us through the thick woods of learning. But exclusive reliance on second-hand things makes second-hand men and women. It deludes us into thinking we are wiser than we are. Our love of digests and books-about-books is a national disease. In the Southwest, not long ago, I saw advertised in all the stores a course in six lectures for those who wanted to become uranium prospectors. There was an opening survey of the atom for those who knew no physics. Breadth of knowledge, even knowing a little about a lot, has its obvious value. But breadth that perpetually sends down no clean, strong roots into the primary sources—into the deep earth and 'the hidden rivers murmuring in the dark' of the rocks—such breadth clarifies very little. It merely puts our bewilderment on a broader basis. It leads us into incredible naïveté and gullibility. It makes us too quick to believe all we read. One remembers Mopsa, the grinning, broad-faced shepherdess of Shakespeare's play, buying all the wares of the ballad-monger and rejoicing, 'I love a ballad in print, a-life, for then we are sure they are true.'

The primary sources are more, however, than mere defenses against error and half-truth. They have a magnificent power of their own—the power of animation and renewal that we can draw on for a lifetime. For they feed streams of living water.

They contain what Van Wyck Brooks has called 'the great themes by virtue of which the race has risen: courage, justice, mercy, honor, love,' the resources 'humanity needs for its survival and perfection.' They bear the mark of enduring things. We can harden our hearts against them, we can forget them in our busyness and aimless rushing about, in all our parasitical existence off what we happen to hear or what somebody happens to tell us. But the primary sources still haunt us and we remember them even against our will, even when 'our backs are turned to the door of our own house.' And suddenly, weary and sick of the commonplace, the meaningless amusements, the second-rate places into which we have slumped down—suddenly, out of the very middle of the lonely crowd, we remember there are other places, places near the deep wells of light and the headwaters of understanding that flow into wisdom and have in themselves a superior deliverance of life.

Thinking of those who have led many a student to the primary places here on this campus, I think also of another former colleague of mine. He was Dean Christian Gauss, of Princeton University, a fine scholar, a beloved teacher, and the stern, warm friend of every underdog that ever crawled into the Dean's office at Nassau Hall. 'An education,' Dean Gauss once said, 'is what you have left after you have lost everything that can possibly be taken away from you.' After most of the ground has slipped from under you, after you and all the others have done you in, after you have lost everything that can be taken away—what then do you have left? That will be your education. And it will be very near the primary sources to which your education has directed you. Thousands of men and women know this is so. To predict that it will be so once more is the best commencement present I know how to give.

It can be so in three ways. The primary sources, the first-hand, permanent stuff that any liberal education can open to one, feed three main areas of our human life. Between birth and death each of us has, it would seem, three great relationships—a relationship with nature and all material objects and the things about us; a relationship with persons, both living and dead; and a relationship with what our idea of the world and life itself can come to be. These are the three great human affairs for all the sons of men. And in every one of them the primary sources are present, with their inexhaustible riches.

The world of nature and objects can be itself a primary source. Education should make it more so. It should give understanding and a lasting love of things for their own good sakes. Too often we are a race of brooders and planners, so busy worrying about our insides and our psychoses, so occupied with what we intend to do tomorrow, that life dies under our feet today. The best men and women I know, with one or two curious exceptions, are those who love the minutiae and detail of existence—to whom a little means a lot. This is a mark, not of triviality but of a real profundity. It is no small thing to possess the world God gave us —to be unwilling to have the wonder of it spoiled by repetition. Indeed, if one cannot possess the world he has, it is very questionable if he deserves another. The night and the morning, the rivers and seas and skies, the curved prows of ships, good wood and old leather and well-wrought glass and silver, flowers and trees and the whole prodigality of earth, white sand and beautiful machines, the life beyond microscope and telescope, the lights and colors and textures of a thousand forms—love some of these in life now if you're keen on immortality.

By all the natural sciences, by art, and music, and literature, and history, and physical education, a college should quicken our perception of these natural primary sources till, like Browning's painter, 'we count it a crime to let one truth slip.' Dr. Alvin Johnson tells us that as a boy he learned the names of two hundred flowering plants and always regarded it as an important stage in his education. 'Without names,' he said, 'you do not see things. You call things gadgets and let it go at that.'

Some of you will remember how Goethe told Eckermann of

his displeasure with many of the 'young learned Germans' who came to see him—how they regarded as 'vain and trivial' the rich detail of things that interested the omniverous Goethe. 'They are,' he complained, 'entirely absorbed in the Idea. . . . Only the highest problems of speculation are fitted to interest them.' He called them 'the young without youth.' 'All youthful feeling and all youthful pleasure are driven out of them and that irrevocably; for if a man is not young in his twentieth year, how can he be so in his fortieth?' Eckermann adds, 'Goethe sighed and was silent.'

The famous Harvard naturalist, Louis Agassiz, was the close friend of William James. Agassiz, James tells us, would excitedly plan the last detail of a journey up the Amazon River or, with equal zest, lock up a student in a room full of shells, without any book or word to help him, and not let him out 'till he had discovered all the truths which the objects contained.' The 'truth of things,' says James, 'is after all their living fullness.' And he would listen with a kind of reverence as Agassiz would quote with deep feeling the lines of *Faust:*

> Gray, dear friend, is all theory,
> And green the golden tree of life.

Before the multifold primary sources, let men cast the scales from their eyes and see into the life of things. How wrong we are to believe that wisdom and faith and the deep things we seek will all come bubbling from our brains as logical propositions. The whole plenitude of God lies all about us unregarded. In his fine poem called 'Reconciliation,' the poet A.E. has this opening line: 'I begin through the grass once again to be bound to the Lord.' In Ireland men knew what he meant. And so, I think, do we.

The second main relationship of our lives carries also its primary sources—the persons who, out of the present and the past, give us strength and substance.

There is
One great society alone on earth:
The noble Living and the noble Dead.

'Like a contagious disease, almost,' it has been said, 'spiritual life passes from man to man by contact.' We are, to an appalling degree, the sum of the human beings our minds possess. We become whom we know. If you were to draw up this morning a list of the people who for you have been the primary sources of your best hours, your list would include both your contemporaries and a heritage out of the past. For some of you, as for me, Abraham Lincoln is much more alive than many of the living. And he, in turn, certainly paid his own acknowledgment to the primary sources on which he drew. How wrong we are to think of him merely as a kind of genius or smart Kentuckian, all horse sense and shrewdness, picking up by instinct all he knew across the cuspidors of a Springfield court house. This tall son of a man who could neither read nor write, whose own formal schooling was actually less than one year, drank long at the deep wells. 'The things I want to know are in books,' he used to say almost in agony, 'and a friend is the man who brings me a book I haven't read.' One cannot forget the picture of Lincoln sitting by the streams near New Salem with his friend Jack Kelso reading Shakespeare to him—the living man and the dead poet both helping him to the high ground of his mind.

There are other symbols of this strange ministry to us of the living and the dead. On summer nights in and near Rome it has become a habit to stage grand opera within the ruined walls of the Baths of Caracalla or the Basilica of Maxentius. Cecil Roberts tells how, one night, hearing the voice of Gigli singing at his best, 'the tall cypresses guarding the horizon of a moonlit world' beyond the Forum, he felt the throng of emperors, philosophers, poets, and orators crowding round out of time. On plain streets in plain cities, in less romantic settings, you and I are doomed to draw daily on the people who stock our minds. It is one of the laws of life that we become the persons who possess us.

Beyond nature, beyond persons living and dead, we all of us have a third relationship—our idea of the world and life itself. As we move into this dimension we start voting. We choose the values, the loyalties, the causes we want to serve. This is the crucial, the ultimate part. And for this, if education opens no primary sources, it is not education at all. For our human culture is no sleek adventure in self-interest, but rather the opening of the mind and heart, under law, to the highest things a man can serve. To say this is not to favor blind and sentimental activity for activity's sake. But it is to recommend reflective commitment, especially now, when our task is not merely to survive, as some think, but to try to find—President Rosemary Park has put it well—'ways of creating out of the wealth of things we have something more than the desire for more things.' It is still the business of good men, by their labor, as George Washington Carver used to say, to 'make Heaven seem a little less problematical.' College graduates have many advantages. But no diploma gives anybody the right to preen and plume himself as if he thought he were the peacock of all culture, or the whipped cream of the human intellect. There is good, hard, dirty work to be done. And if a man doesn't decide to do some of it in his time, nature will soon say to him, 'Son, either paint or get off the ladder.' Gandhi once wrote, 'I am familiar with the superstition that self-realization is possible only in the fourth stage of life, i.e., *sannyasa* (renunciation). But it is a matter of common knowledge that those who defer preparation for this invaluable experience until the last stage of life attain not self-realization but old age.' You will remember Bunyan's immortal Captain who stepped up to the Keeper of the Book of Life and said, 'Put my name down, Sir.' At that moment the primary sources open with joy.

A man is not born with the arts and sciences of a high civilization, as Walter Lippmann has recently reminded us. He acquires them by attending to the conquests of the human spirit over many generations. It is sometimes a slow and painful business, and the way seems very long. And, as he struggles, there are many voices telling him that our deliverance comes quite another way —not from the hard-won primary sources but from a primitivism that recognizes in man only the basic impulses of his raw nature and his subconsciousness. But in his best moments a man can still see that 'something in us,' as Rufus Jones used to say, 'did not originate in the world of matter, in the time-space order. . . . We are more than biological exhibits. We have a spiritual lineage. We may have collateral connections with flat-nosed baboons . . . but we belong to an Overworld of a higher order.' 'Someday,' he continues, 'the deeps below the deeps will be found, and there in the darkness and quiet we shall come on impressive and convincing proof of Him who dwells both in the darkness and the light.'

And the ultimate primary thing is simply this: the stunning love of God that nothing can stop. *His* love I am talking about. Not ours. The love of God is endless. This College was built that men might be told just that, in the hope that sooner or later they might believe it. Years ago when his contemporaries marveled at the life of Savonarola—at all the good things he thought and did —they asked him how he got that way. His answer was a simple one: 'A word did it.' A college ought to give a man that word.

The well of Jacob was a deep well in the land of Samaria. The water was clear and cool, and had been so for many generations. It seemed entirely adequate. Then one day a man came to sit by it and spoke with a woman. And from that day the well, the woman, and all her friends were changed. For He spoke of water they had never tasted, that springs up into everlasting life. He did not say that He was just another man, a new philosopher with a beautiful thought. He said He was the Son of God. And the woman and her friends believed Him, saying: 'We have heard Him ourselves and know that this is the Christ, the Saviour of the World.' And when His disciples found Him, he wasn't even hungry. 'I have meat to eat that ye know not of. It is to do the will of Him that sent me, and to finish the work.'

# The *Not* So Lonely Crowd
## (1957)

Four years ago, when the class we honor tomorrow was graduating from school, it was no uncommon June. The Korean War was ending. A Queen of England had just been crowned, and the world's highest mountain, conquered for the first time, lay at her feet as a coronation jewel. A young switch-hitter named Mickey Mantle was showing signs of promise and had made the cover of *Time* magazine. At a moment when commencement orators were pouring advice over the green land, an older ball player, one Satchel Paige, was giving to the public for the first time his secret rules for staying young: 'Avoid fried meats, which angry up the blood. Avoid running at all times. And don't look back. Something might be gaining on you.'

Then, in September of that same year of 1953, the very week that certain freshmen were checking into Wooster, groaning at the new rules and discovering how much joy can go out of life when the Presbyterians get hold of it, a professor at the University of Illinois was asking loudly, 'What is memory?' Hardly waiting for an answer, he announced that no one knew at all how the brain, with its ten billion neurons, stores up information. This chilling mystery was not revealed to the freshmen at convocation that fall, and they, in four years, have not fully solved the problem either.

But on this new June morning, as we welcome the parents and families and friends of the class of 1957, we suggest that you defy both the old ball player and the doctor—that you do look back, trust your memory, whatever it may be, and freely rejoice, along with us, in your sons and daughters. It is a relaxed moment. Once again we have signed the diplomas in advance, as a kind of vote for predestination. So, one day short of commencement, let pride and gratitude and affection make up the warmth of this family occasion. It is a shining hour, and a moving one, even for those of us who have been here many years.

In that summer of 1953 a new analysis of contemporary life was in its fifth printing. The book was called *The Lonely Crowd*, and something about it rang like either a warning or a tolling bell in the minds of thoughtful readers. For David Riesman, the sociologist at the University of Chicago, and his collaborators spoke of a new form of the spiritual loneliness of man, of a new and quite literal kind of *self*-destruction. They wrote not as preachers or moralists, but as wise, urbane, and very modest social scientists, reporting a new aspect of human behavior and its growing result. To many who listened, the 'lonely crowd' seemed very real. And, in this analysis, it seemed something new.

The loneliness of man is, of course, no new thing. He has long known it on the desert or the sea, in mountain solitude, or in the face of the silent stars. He is quite aware of what death is, and unrequited love, and the benumbing failures in human communication. He has been down the blind alleys and has wandered, as a solitary, between the two worlds of doubt and faith. He has had in his time the shock of Copernicus and Darwin and the news of the dark caverns of his own subconscious mind. On the lonely plains of the West he has heard, not just the coyote's cry in the night and the old, classic sounds of isolation, but a violent noise of nature split in two and has seen the strange stark clouds in the sky full of a frightening, ambiguous rain. He has known the loneliness even of abject and slavish fear, and in many places of the earth has enacted that metaphor of Mr. Lippmann's that a British critic calls one of the 'tremendous metaphors' of our time—when a whole society or nation will 'welcome manacles to prevent its hands shaking.' So man has felt bereft of home; but this bereavement is ancient in the world, one way or another, and the gods still give, as in Homer's time, 'an enduring heart to the children of men.'

And the crowd itself, as an experience, is not new. The industrial revolution well behind him, man is quite used to size and multitudes. Bigness itself no longer scares him. E. B. White, one of New York City's prime gifts to civilization, believes that about the only real community of the city—'the only event that hits every New Yorker on the head'—is the St. Patrick's Day Parade. But in the stone caverns of Manhattan, Mr. White finds all manner of spiritual wealth. Indeed, he says that New York can confer a positive 'gift of loneliness,' a 'gift of privacy' to anyone who can receive it. Nor is he defeated by the big statistics. We are told, he says, that 'the Long Island Railroad alone carried forty million commuters last year; but many of them were the same fellow retracing his steps.' Or a man can sit, for example, in a huge stadium of a hundred thousand souls and soon begin to feel he has no special identity or soul at all. But let him then think, as the poet bids him, of another crowd in a cathedral setting, touched by music and reverence and beauty, and he can quickly conquer the loneliness of mere numbers, aware that there can be a 'dignity in a concourse of men' when 'some spiritual gleam hearteneth the herd.'

The 'lonely crowd,' as Mr. Riesman sees it, is quite another matter. This is a phenomenon belonging especially to our time. We have given it at least a new lease on life. For the 'lonely crowd' is not composed of men and women who take their direction from a tradition or from goals and standards inwardly held as their own possession. It is made up, rather, of those whom Mr.

Riesman calls the 'other-directed' people. What they have in common is that their contemporaries alone are the source of all their direction—either contemporaries they actually know or those they have heard about 'through friends or the mass media.' They come mostly from the upper-middle classes of our larger cities. But they are spreading, and much of our education fosters their development. They acquire a quick and almost psychic response to what they think of as a 'peer group,' and their passion in life is to please. Their 'other-directedness' is not that of the healthy extrovert who is just naturally a nice, outgoing fellow to start with. Neither does it represent any solid love or concern for a neighbor or a community. It reflects rather a very anxious desire for immediate approval, for giving the calculated 'glad hand' in conformity to the right group—a desire to be 'well-adjusted' and to 'get along.' There are no dearly bought long-range goals, nor great men summoned from out the past as models. The password is 'now' and very heaven is to be 'accepted.' This is their god, their goal, their benzedrine.

Mr. Riesman is very sensible and dispassionate about all this. He has too much knowledge and too much humor to be a label-paster. He sees all of us, at various times in our lives, moving freely among the categories. He never equates 'inner direction,' for example, with conscience, and reminds us that 'a scoundrel who knows what he aims for can be as unequivocally inner-directed as a God-fearing puritan.' He thinks it no crime for men to want to be liked. He is not angry at the big advertisers, the man in the gray flannel suit, the public-relations boys, the junior executive, the 'corporation man,' or at big business. In fact, he wishes that educators could give students something more than the fixed notion that the only choice in life is 'making money (and losing one's soul) in business versus penury (and saving one's soul) in government service or teaching.' He wishes students had a better image of the 'challenging intellectual problems' of big business and its opportunities. If they do not acquire it, he says, 'business will be forced to recruit from the less gifted and sensitive, who will muff their opportunities.' No, Mr. Riesman is not out to 'get' anyone.

But the overtones of his book are clear. What he cannot conceal is his concern about this growing 'lonely crowd' in our American culture. They are lonely because the return, the spiritual enjoyment, on their lives is so thin. They lack values and inner resources and have no authentic life of their own. They 'use the noise of the others to drown the noise of the self.' They have no chart, no compass, and no anchor. They feel, not guilt but only a series of small anxieties. Even their 'sphere of pleasures has become a sphere of cares.' They have no grand and noble aspirations to weigh or measure by. Their passion in life is to be properly 'adjusted,' and they waste their days 'adjusting' themselves to things not worth being adjusted to. All this breeds sleekness without fibre—and ennui and, at the last, a solitary chill about the heart. Mr. Riesman, of course, puts this more scientifically: if these 'other-directed people should discover how much needless work they do, discover that their own thoughts and their own lives are quite as interesting as other people's, that, indeed, they no more assuage their loneliness in a crowd of peers than one can assuage one's thirst by drinking sea water, then we might expect them to become more attentive to their own feelings and aspirations.' Such is the new loneliness, on a growing mass scale. It is the assembly line of the inwardly bereft. And the worst of it is, that it is a fashionable kind of loneliness—a loneliness that men are not just resigning to. They are making up to it, asking for it, as they join the lonely crowd.

I can think of no better wish a college could give its graduates than this—that they may have membership in 'the *not* so lonely crowd' all the days of their lives. There is a way of deliverance from the spiritual poverty of the lonely crowd itself. Something can be done. And this something is, if realized, perhaps the best fruit of a college education. It demands standing both inside and outside the crowd of mankind and bringing to the human situation some very definite things.

What is first demanded is a touch of common sense about the crowd itself, of which we all are part. There must be no snobbery about the vulgar herd. If a college education breeds a contemptuous superiority, a refined disdain, it has failed of its purpose. Anyone who watched as I did last summer for a full day seven hundred rescued souls from the *Andrea Doria*, many stunned by their loss of everything but their lives, will never have to be coached again about the rich and incredible resources of human nature. Men and women, with and without formal education, are inexhaustible in their capacity to furnish the surprises of the soul. To appreciate this is essential.

Some more common sense helps us to avoid turning ourselves over to major-league loneliness or brooding about ourselves too much. By doing some honest work the best we can do it, by minding our own business and the job at hand, by loving a few friends and the renewing beauty of each common day, by having at least one good cause that we utterly serve, we can do much for ourselves. Do you remember Homer Jack's account of Albert Schweitzer at Lambarene in Africa—filling his days with the chores at the hospital, supervising a new building, answering correspondence from all over the world, looking to the welfare of some three thousand patients a year and about three hundred resident lepers? Then 'at six o'clock, in the fast descending twilight —for the hospital is only forty miles south of the equator—Dr. Schweitzer often leaves his study with one antelope on leash. He gets a respite from the day's activities by sitting down on a concrete block and looking over the palms to the wide Ogowe River and toward the town of Lambarene around the bend beyond. Natives are crossing the river silently in their dug-out canoes.' Do you suppose that this man, one of the great, learned, talented men of all time, ever thinks of these people he serves or of himself, either, as part of some 'lonely crowd'?

But common sense alone—humility, work, deep attachment to

others—will not wholly suffice us. There is a depth in us that calls for recognition. It demands to be touched by the best that man knows. And it is this best that man knows that the lonely crowd has turned away from, just as a man turns away from the door of his own house.

The best that man knows is something more than the understanding of one's self that comes from psychology or psychiatry, valuable as these are. It is, indeed, absurd to scorn them. Surely the professional counselor who knows his business is better than the well-intended but blundering amateur whose efforts often remind one of the tender-hearted elephant that, meeting some motherless chicks in a forest, said, 'Don't worry little ones. I'll be a mother to you,' and sat down on them. Yet, even so, psychiatry is not a total deliverer. As the reviewer of T. S. Eliot's play so brilliantly saw, 'the psychiatrist can explain life; he cannot give it meaning.' What one needs is some Idea of the world—something that can inform and direct life and lend it significance. Adjustment to this is the superb and crucial adjustment. This goes leagues beyond the little law of averages, the little rules of social and commercial acceptance, that haunt the lonely crowd. What one longs to hear from men's lips is not just 'My analyst tells me—' but 'My synthesist tells me.' This world of the best man knows contains the luminous ideas and commanding values that give us center and direction. These ideas confer a power of high and noble action and commitments that span more than one small, strategic day. They reflect the heritage that is our only answer to the barbarities of our time—what Clifton Fadiman has called 'the ideas, the visions, the laughter, the deep cries of anguish, the great Eurekas of revelation that make up our patent to the title of civilized man.'

This College holds that the highest of these great ideas was the Word made flesh in the life and death and resurrection of our Lord Jesus Christ. As do all who hold such faith, it believes that this is the way of both identification and transcendence, the ultimate way out of the 'lonely crowd.' I cannot, in honesty, give a baccalaureate invitation to something better than the lonely crowd without saying, as simply and bluntly as I can, that the superb love of God, made real for us in His Son, is the ultimate sense of this whole matter. I know nothing else that stands up so high or goes so deep, nothing else that answers at every point to the dark recesses and the bright reaches of both the inward and the outward life. This is the ground on which the humblest and the most sophisticated soul can, trusting the inexhaustible love and mercy of God, despise the short marches, the early surrenders, the picayune adjustments, the tiny diplomacies. On this ground a man can know the best that there is. He can bet his life on the long causes, the long loyalties, the generous community of free men that rises above the lonely crowd.

On December 12th of last year the *Queen Mary* was bound for New York and running late, delayed by heavy seas. There was still a chance that she might make port on the scheduled day, with her cargo of Christmas goods and mail. Suddenly there came a call from the little Panamanian freighter, the *Santa Ana*, saying that her captain had a dangerous nose-bleed and needed medical help—maybe even surgery. Promptly the *Queen Mary* turned her vast bulk off her course. She sped to the rescue of the ailing seaman, hauled him aboard, and gave him the care that saved his life, losing two hours and eight minutes and clinching her late arrival in New York. Somehow in the dark of the illimitable ocean one thought a great deal of this, and concluded, with exhilaration, that the machine still loses on occasion in its long contest with the human heart. That winter night the ships of the North Atlantic were not tracking the broad sea as a lonely crowd. They were a significant community. For the rudder of the *Queen Mary* was not making an adjustment to the waiting shops of New York, the dinners and theaters cancelled on shore, or the fuming of impatient passengers. It was fixed rather to the high codes that should govern civilized men.

It seems to me that the two eyes of history will find an unspoken relationship between that action and the Sunday morning that preceded it. On that morning these same ship's officers, with the passengers, the stewards and the stewardesses, the doctors and nurses and the little page boys, their white gloves tucked on top of the shoulder, had read together the service of the Church of England. They had come to that ship from the towns and villages and the churches that still bless the countryside of Great Britain. Many times over the years they had read from the Prayer Book those unchanging words. As Charles Morgan reminds us, in his *Reflections in a Mirror*, every phrase in that Prayer Book was a familiar emblem. 'It is wonderfully comprehensive. One would venture to say that there is no human need, spiritual or temporal, that is not remembered in it. The word "all" rings through it like a bell. "All that are in danger . . . all that travel by land or by water . . . all sick persons and young children . . . all prisoners and captives . . . all that are desolate and oppressed." Nothing and no one is forgotten. Everyone in the congregation may hear prayed for that one being on earth who lies nearest his heart. . . . It is all said. It was written yesterday, today, and tomorrow. As the necessities of men change, and from youth to age or from generation to generation their joys and sufferings alter their forms and names, the words of the Litany open to include them.'

Out of such benediction arises the high fellowship of the 'Not So Lonely Crowd.'

# The Big World
## (1958)

It is always hard to choose the last word you want a college to give to those who leave it. But this year I had no problem. Our theme this morning was almost forced on me—as early as last Christmas—by the conjunction of four ideas and images that seemed to come together out of those exciting days. If, at the start, you will think with me on this four-part collision, you will at least understand the accident itself and quickly be on the ground of our thought this morning.

The first part was the International Geophysical Year, as interesting to many of you as it has been to me. This attempt of scientists to cross the boundaries of many nations in a common civility of knowledge and inquiry, which we might well emulate in other areas of our life, has stretched our minds into new awareness of time and space, and of the staggering universe in which we live. Years ago Alfred Tennyson thought of his Creator as 'boundless inward in the atom, boundless outward in the whole'—in a volume entitled *Locksley Hall, Sixty Years After, etc.* And now, sixty-two years after that, it is the 'et cetera' that is magnificent. Magnificent in the inner space that is made solid energy by whirling electrons moving round nuclei at incredible speed; while the mind, on its outward run, can see through 2000 million light-years of space and recover something of the very creation of the stars. Beyond the Milky Way, and its own 100 billion stars, are the 'two populations' of the other galaxies, and the Andromeda Nebula. Far down below us are the vast trenches of the ocean floor that make the canyons we know look like gullies. And the human race, which, as a scientific friend reminds me, could be put in a box of one cubic mile and dropped into a vast expanse of 329 million cubic miles of sea, refuses to be so tiny, and from its little spot of earth keeps its steady cosmic quest and, just for exercise, pitches its own bright satellites into the night.

There was a second moment of realization, at Christmas time, when we waited for three cold evenings on the hills in the hope of seeing a Sputnik that eluded us, thought of another star that men once went out to see, and came home to read before a bright fire and a Christmas tree orbiting its own gay satellites as if it, too, were joining in the Geophysical Year.

And the book I read had in it a poem of Robert Frost long dear to me. In a New England winter evening, the night falling fast, the traveler sees the lanes and fields and woods filling with the sudden snow. There is an obliterating whiteness, as the familiar landmarks fade away—and loneliness of the deeper sort. And the poet cries: *

> They cannot scare me with their empty spaces
> Between stars—on stars where no human race is.
> I have it in me so much nearer home
> To scare myself with my own desert places.

That is the third part; the fourth part came shortly after. I was reading the life of Sir Henry Jones by H. J. W. Hetherington, the Principal of the University of Glasgow. Sir Henry is writing to his son away in Burma: 'Feed your soul a little when you get the chance with the fine things. For it is the invisible world of motives and purposes, and ends, and will and justice, and loving-kindness—that is the big world, and not the mere shell we see.'

And so, out of the Geophysical Year, the satellite, the traveler facing the problem of our own empty inner space on a New England road, and a brave letter to a far-off son, I knew what I wanted the final word of the College to be this morning—that there is, authentically, a big world open to our possession, a fullness of life that men and women can have, not out in the galaxies, but here on the earth we live on, in the life we know. And I want you, if you will, to think of what prevents this big world, of what fosters it, and its particular problem at the moment for you and me.

What is it that does spoil the big world and prevents our having it? So many things, and every person here knows part of them. I have no wish to parade our common faults this morning, lest we begin to look like Eden six hours after the snake arrived. But we all know how he got there. And the worst of what he left was pride—pride that can put a stranglehold upon us all. Pride that makes us want things for all the wrong reasons—because our neighbors or the Russians have them. Pride that sent the lady to the symphony in Kansas City, where David Riesman heard her sigh, at the end of a Philharmonic series, 'Thank goodness, that's over.' When he asked her why, feeling as she did, she went to concerts at all, she replied, 'Well, Dallas has a symphony orchestra, and so does St. Louis!' Pride that keeps us from entering many a world of knowledge and delight because we are afraid to admit our ignorance or to acknowledge we are behindhand or have lost our way. A modern critic much admires the sentence with which Matthew Arnold began, at the age of nearly sixty-five—in America he would have been retired—his essay on the French journalist Amiel: 'It is somewhat late to speak of Amiel, but I was late in reading him.' That is the humble, honest way. It is also the learned, Olympian way. Except you become as a little child, you do not enter the kingdoms of either earth or Heaven.

There are, thank goodness, the forces that work against the shrinking of our lives—that work for the big world and not against it. And a liberal education ought to be one of them. Do you remember how Woodrow Wilson, one of the best of teachers, used to put it: 'It would be a very petty life to live if we were merely schoolmasters; it would not interest me for twenty-four hours to be a taskmaster in respect to the studies of a lot of youngsters. Unless I can lead them to see the beauty of the things that have seemed beautiful to me, I have mistaken my profession. It is not the whip that makes men, but the lure of things that are worthy to be loved.' Such is the way to the big world.

But in 1958 all education, liberal or otherwise, isn't worth much unless we solve some very specific human problems that bedevil us just now. One of these is the short-changing of ourselves by making the word 'security' not the important word it rightly is, but the main word, the top goal that discounts the high risks that have always ennobled men and women. Life doesn't belong, of course, to the uncalculating fool and the facile optimist. But neither does it belong to the facile pessimist, who can win an easy reputation for soundness and profundity merely by carrying an automatic Flit gun in his brain. 'Looking for fleas in the lion's mane,' as someone said, is no way to spend all twenty-four hours of a given day. The big world does not readily open to those who have succumbed to the law of averages, the kind of statistical determinism that cancels the dynamic spirit of men. Do you remember, in this connection, Webster's fine cartoon, showing the bridge expert, with Goren in his hand, saying to the couple who have just taken the game, 'You wouldn't have won if you'd played it right.'

Even the great men have had to keep their courage, and it's nice to know that they do. Sir Winston Churchill has been called our nearest reincarnation of the Renaissance man. 'Certainly for sheer virtuosity we have not seen his equal in our time.' Yet, at the recent exhibition of his paintings, one reads again of the Sunday morning he started to paint in oils, when he knew not where or how to begin, and his 'hand seemed arrested by a silent veto.' With a tiny brush and tremendous caution he made at last, in the area where he knew the sky ought to be, a blue mark 'about as big as a bean.' Then he stopped. And his career as a painter might have stopped, had not Sir John Laverty's wife arrived at the moment, asked for a bigger brush, and, with 'large, fierce strokes,' proved to him that the canvas 'could not hit back.' And his hand reached forth to possess a new and wonderful world.

The 'hand arrested by a silent veto.' This spirit of negation did not stop the pioneers. Alfred Kazin believes that the great theme of Willa Cather's novels is 'the struggle between grandeur and meanness, the two poles of her world. . . . She did not celebrate the pioneer as such; she sought his image in all creative spirits— explorers and artists, lovers and saints, who seemed to live by a purity of aspiration.' Likewise, 'the old pioneer grandfather in Steinbeck's *The Long Valley*, remembering the brutality of men on the great trek, also remembered enough of its glory to say: "It wasn't the Indians that were important, nor adventures, nor even getting out here. . . . When we saw the mountains at last, we cried—all of us. But it wasn't getting here that mattered, it was movement and westering. We carried life out here and set it down the way those ants carry eggs. . . . The westering was as big as God, and the slow steps that made the movement piled up and piled up until the continent was crossed." '

Some of the pioneers stay at home, and make a big world of their own few acres, the familiar ground. By some singular gift of imagination they translate into significance the tract of land below their sky. Thoreau did it at Walden, the Brontës on the Yorkshire moors, Wordsworth in the English Lakes, Charles Lamb in London. People can make 'a great heart within a little house' till their names are mentioned in the travel bureaus only in whispers lest they spoil the trade. And I see no reason this morning why I should not mention a friend whom I have admired a long time. This June our community will celebrate its one hundred fiftieth anniversary, and no one has been the moving spirit of its preparation more than Arthur Miller has. Beyond what was once a rubbish dump and on what were barren hills, he has made life grow into what a discriminating visitor and much-traveled man described as one of the most distinguished places he had ever seen. The creation of a new world on one's home acres is not just a matter of having the means and the right bulldozers at hand. Trees and lakes and flowers in inspired proportion spring from the imagination, such as this man has in vast measure. And so, looking back upon it, it seems not too strange now that his son—a member of the class of 1941, a boy so many people loved—did what he did one afternoon some months ago. In charge of a loading operation up by Lake Erie, he saw a workman slipping down into a huge pile of loose slag. Straight as an arrow from his own heart's bow, he leaped in to save him, losing his own life, proving as much as anything else that he was his father's son. On the home ground, in one's little world that the mind and the soul can touch and transform, the big world can come. For out of the heart, as always, are the issues of life.

But in the summer of 1958, we are all somehow called by our destiny, because we happen to be living now, into a larger world. It should be the concern of every man—beyond his home ground. On a June morning I am not launching a panel discussion on international affairs. I have never subscribed, indeed, to the notion that if the world isn't saved by commencement, it won't be saved at all. Don Marquis used to say that 'economic problems that cannot otherwise be solved should be abolished.' But it isn't that easy. The anthropologists sense that 'we who are now alive are passing through an age of transition, the first major cultural shift since the Neolithic began about 6000 B.C.' Man, who learned to speak and warm himself, to cook and sew, to hunt, and cultivate and invent, is now in a new phase—he has learned to waste the materials of earth and to destroy himself. His present task is, not just political unification, but all that lies behind the possibility of political success—the conservation of resources, the control of population, the right use of brain power. Dr. Carleton Coon, who brilliantly analyzes this situation, thinks the heart of the problem is simply the cultural lag between our invention and our wisdom, and that our greatest need is humility and, at the same time, a new declaration of the importance of the individual. Beyond atomic war and the erosion of the earth is the failure of the peoples of the earth, of different cultural backgrounds, to understand each other, especially when seven hundred million people in eighteen nations have just tasted freedom for the first time. This is the tough task of our day. And the big world will be the little world—the ominously dangerous world—till this gets done.

Part of whatever wisdom we attain will come, as so much of life comes, from whatever faith is in us. And the fact that we think this will not come as news, either, to the class of 1958. I believe we have honestly tried to show them, especially this year, that the divers faiths of the world—Buddhism, Islam, Hinduism, and the rest—have been full of the spirit that strives toward God. We can learn much from faiths that are not our own. And tomorrow morning we shall give a sound diploma even to anyone who has no faith at all. We have no religious test for graduation. But we do want something better for a man than his own bootstraps, something better than drugs, and drink, and 'ordinary sex,' and a submission to the herd instinct, Communist or Fascist, that Aldous Huxley rates as the favorite forms of escapism just now. We want the big world to include more than even the wonderful heritage we have out of Greece and Rome. We want it to include more than even the love of ideas alone, and the analysis and names of things, lest we become like Phillips Brooks's train caller of whom David Redding, one of our graduates, told us. The temptation of the train caller is the temptation of ministers and teachers and college presidents. He had cried out 'the destination of life so many times, that he was betrayed into thinking he had himself been to the place about which he recited.' We want it to include a life of thought and feeling and action of the kind Paul found in the deeper reality of a Lord who was what He said He was: the

Son of the Living God. Rooted and grounded in love, Paul found himself able to comprehend the 'breadth, and length, and depth, and height,' and was 'filled with all the fulness of God.'

Men have always gone to school in the night above their heads. Some have found the frightening silence of the infinite spaces; some, the hint of the moral law; some, the sense of the Love that moves the sun and the other stars. The Milky Way, with its hundred million points of light, speaks nightly to the high part of our imagination. But it speaks less, I dare assert, than the great windows of King's College Chapel at Cambridge, the most complete series of ancient windows in the world. There in blazoned glass is history—the rose of Lancaster and York and the Tudors, the Hawthorn Bush of Bosworth Field, the fleur-de-lis and the red dragon. The angels and prophets are there, the old law and the new. And the golden calf, the Queen of Sheba, Cain killing Abel, Job tormented, the flight into Egypt, the life of our Lord and His Lady Mother, and Pilate washing his hands. There is also a death and an arising. These windows know more than the stars know or seem to tell.

But we do not know them, as long as they stay in windows. The big world does not live in stars and glass and stone. It must come down from the stars and the windows into the hearts of men—into their hands and their heads—till they have all the boldness of life, transformed by the love of very God Himself. This is the size of the life you want for your sons and daughters —not just happiness, and success, and health—but a creative life of meaning and real worth. And a college has the right to want it for them too.

Earlier this morning I remarked that it was always hard to choose the last word that a college said to its graduates. And suddenly I realized that it isn't hard to choose at all. The last word is said tomorrow. As you walk to receive your diploma the Dean will pronounce your name—even the hard middle names. It is disconcerting to find somebody you have known as a good plain fellow for four years turning up at graduation with a middle name like 'Theophilus.'

But this is what we give you as the last word—your own name. And you can make that, if you want to, a better thing than any diploma any college can put in your hands. You can take it out from here and set it down in the big world and know what work and love and joy are till the day you die. And when you get tired and want renewal, come back here to the old ivory tower. We shall let you gripe and sign petitions and write letters to the college paper and break off your heels in the brick walks and feel young again. And, strange as it may seem to you, we shall not remember your failures. We shall remember the youth and the life and goodness and beauty you brought here in your time. We are very grateful for all that. We are even more grateful for what you may yet become.

# To What Green Altar?
## (1959)

Among the silent forms that mark the side of John Keats's 'Grecian Urn,' is the vignette of those coming to the sacrifice out of some little town 'by river or seashore' in time long gone:

> To what green altar, O mysterious priest,
> Lead'st thou that heifer lowing at the skies,
> And all her silken flanks with garlands drest?

This is the question that has recurred to me for over thirty years. With almost humorous frequency, has come this image of the green altar in the primal woods in the early morning of the world. With repetition it has grown into a symbol. It stands somehow for whatever is truly living, for whatever is fresh and unspoiled. It is the quiet place in a noisy time, the shining hour in a dull day. It is the place of truth and goodness and beauty for which the mind yearns and the soul aspires. It is the shrine of any faith we have, to which we bring the best we know.

'To what green altar?' It is a rebuke to the brittle and undiscerning hours when the mind stays stupid and the soul won't budge—when custom conquers and wonder dies. The rebuke to the job not done with all one's power and the good moment bungled; to the cause not served, the word not spoken, the wrong not righted. The rebuke to the short-range answers to long-range questions, to mechanical action and imagination laid low. Wherever life is less than life should be the demanding voice arises: 'To what green altar bring you these dead things?'

So this morning I share this haunting question with you. It has meaning for baccalaureate morning. For graduates of a college are, beyond their own power to resign, the privileged people of their generation. In a world that does not always value intelligence, they have incurred an obligation to be aware. They are supposed to stand up for the mind, to bring to the green altars of life the gift of living ideas, ideas that live and move as fresh water does or as the color moves and flows in the sunlight in the luminous windows of Chartres.

The mere possession of ideas is only a beginning. It is their quality that counts, the way they are arrived at and held, the vitality they keep. A man may be trained in logical thought, know any number of facts, be familiar with the best critical methods, and still have no ideas that live for him. One of our best thinkers recalls the *New Yorker*'s account of the man who was asked if he had read a certain Book-of-the-Month Club book and answered, 'Not personally.' Ideas can be held that way, not as animating possession but as dead catalogue. And when they are, they are not fit to be laid on the green altars of life.

Moreover, ideas are dangerous when they lie in the head like debris. Some of you know my admiration for T. S. Eliot's fine praise of Henry James for 'his mastery over, his baffling escape from, Ideas; a mastery and an escape which are perhaps the last test of a superior intelligence. He had a mind so fine that no idea could violate it.' This implies no treason to thinking, to information, nor even to those 102 ideas one office at the University of Chicago once catalogued as the ideas possible to man—nor to those self-evident, eternal truths to which we are all bound, the 'blazing ubiquities,' as Emerson called them.

But it does imply that one of the tasks of liberal education is to save us from the tyranny of the floating concepts that, detached from life and history and human depth, can become our terrible masters. We have a facility, and some men have a positive genius, for turning the luminous words, the inexhaustible words that should never 'harden and grow cold'—words like liberty, rights, duties, security, nationalism, goodness, truth, beauty, and even love—into catch phrases of such tiny meaning and corrupt application that they enslave the mind and constitute a danger both to the individual and to the state. Ideas can be 'correct' and yet so detached from presiding principle that they lie like polished marbles on the shelf of the brain. One thinks, somehow, of Voltaire, whose mind went everywhere, just as he himself 'darted about Europe like a nervous fish in a tank.' His wit was sharpened to the finest edge, and his prose was like his mind—lucid and strong. His superb brain seemed to compensate for his puny body. As was said of him, 'He was born with one foot in the grave and sustained that asymmetrical position for eighty-four years.' In fifty-two fat volumes of some thirty thousand pages, brilliant as they are, something seems missing, some detachment from informing principle and central depth. He seems in too many places to prefer 'truth of the triumphant sort,' the quick victories of the intellect rather than the breath and finer spirit of all knowledge. As one with a turn for paradox and a really startling insight has said, the fifty-two volumes are 'a chaos of clear ideas.'

It is the fortune of liberal education, which honors ideas, that it also furnishes the means to ventilate them in the perspective of living truth and experience. It brings them to the bar of great example. It reminds us that ideas compete, that they can be correct and still inadequate, that they can stay beyond their time, and that some of them must be waited for till the right hour comes. It recognizes that ideas receive both their fullness and correction out of the depth and breadth that is the glory of liberal learning. This is the road that leads us to the green altars of life where we bring the best that we know.

What makes for living ideas, ideas really adequate for life? How can we increase our chance of having them? We can do this in many ways—first of all, by relating the ideas we do have to the common sense of humanity. For the common sense of humanity, whatever its faults may be, has a deep regard for ultimate fact. For that matter, it has a deep regard for education. It does not join in the vicious anti-intellectualism of our time. But it does not lightly suffer educated fools. It has disdain for posturing and conceit. It does not wish to be taken in. It can be temporarily fooled and follow many a vain show, but it has a built-in capacity for returning to what is so. It has its own salty test for truth. The lanky old fellow in 'Abe Martin's' drawings used to remark that when you hear a fellow say that it isn't the money but the principle of the thing, 'it's the money.' Some sense of this deep human reservoir informed the idealism of Emerson. This is why he preferred the true scholar or Man Thinking to the book-worm—the pedant, the art-for-art's-sake aesthete, or the professional highbrow, whom A. P. Herbert once defined as 'the kind of person who looks at a sausage and thinks of Picasso.' The true scholar, says Emerson, 'loses no hour which the man lives.' As a kind of graduating present, let me give you his wonderful wisdom: 'Every man I meet is my master in some point, and in that I learn of him.'

This human world on which the true scholar draws is not just the world, of course, of one's own town or one's own country. It is the total human fellowship of East and West throughout the earth. Lovely as 'our town' is, it is no longer enough. Nor is our century, or our own generation. Out of the humane past and its wisdom, out of both 'the noble living and the noble dead' come whatever vision of greatness we may know in our own time upon the earth. One of the dangers of too strong an effort to make learning always 'student-centered' and 'related to life' in too narrow a way is that it may be related to too small a life and a center that isn't center at all. Education is a 'drawing out' and its business is not merely to confirm a man in what he already knows and to exalt his own immediate preferences and predilections. 'Your enlightenment,' Woodrow Wilson used to say, 'depends on the company you keep. You do not know the world until you

know the men who have possessed it and tried its ways before
ever you were given your brief run upon it. And there is no san-
ity comparable to that which is schooled in the thoughts that will
keep.' The green altars are out of all time.

We have a second way of keeping ideas alive—by not suc-
cumbing to the forms and pressures of our day. To the concept
of bigness regarded as a value, to exaggeration of machinery and
material comfort as an end in itself, or to that subtle flattery of
the mediocre which is the perversion of democracy. Henry Commager reminds us that 'every time-saving machine requires another to fill the time that has been saved.' Personally, I believe we
have much more general intelligence in America than we had
thirty years ago. Nevertheless, the words Aldous Huxley wrote
in 1927 are still so. He believed, you will remember, that the machinery which creates leisure and multiplies the number of im-
pressions men and women can receive increases the chance of a
rich universal culture. Yet, he confessed, people can still 'live out
their lives without once being solitary, without once making a
serious mental effort . . . without once being out of sight or
sound of some ready-made distraction.' Even the occasional
viewer of television gets the impression that America's chief business is glutting and guzzling and then recovering in some high bi-
carbonate fashion by taking something that acts twice as fast as
something else. Television's nightly brooding over our digestive
tract reminds me somehow of George Chappell's satirical book of
years ago entitled, *Through the Alimentary Canal with Gun and
Camera.* Excellence is still not a commodity to be bought at every
corner store. It is still not 'common and abundant.' It 'dwells
among rocks hardly accessible, and a man must almost wear his
heart out' in search of it. Strait is the gate, and narrow is the way
that leads to life—to the quiet places and the green altars.

A third way to bring ideas to life is relating them to practical
affairs—to reflective commitments and to causes, large and small,

that deserve to command our loyalty. The educated person rightly learns to suspend judgment, to seek out both sides of a case, to lower his voice and modulate his mind. But in many areas of life he has no license to be anemic, to be forever learning, never coming to a knowledge of the truth. Nor has the academic world a right to make a profession of being slow to get the point of a few plain matters. A man can be drenched with sweetness and light and wear all the adornments of liberal learning, but if, at some point, he does not take his stand on a few compelling principles, his ideas, like the rest of him, will not live. As some of you know, I regard Lionel Trilling as the finest critic I happen to read. He is a lover of beauty and truth and fine distinctions. But he loves goodness also. Listen to his measured words: 'Surely the great work of our time is the restoration and the reconstruction of the will.'

Tolerance is a great virtue, and our modern stress upon it was overdue. But we can make a fetish of tolerance and pervert it into moral cowardice and insipidity. We can, as Peter Marshall used to say, fall for everything until we stand for nothing.

'I had come to the great healing last chapter of *The Brothers Karamazov*,' wrote Alexander Woollcott in a playful letter. 'It always chokes me up and fills me with a love of mankind which sometimes lasts till noon of the following day.' Till noon of the following day is no proper measure for the high passions you and I now have some obligation to feel. And the end of liberal learning is not merely to give us the ground of making intelligent choice among many possibilities. It should strengthen also the moral force that makes the choices stick. How can a man who really loves ideas be indifferent to cruelty and injustice and what disfigures life?

You must have been moved, as I was, if you read the other day Norman Cousins's account in the *Saturday Review* of a brutal incident in the Stamford railway station. It was a Sunday evening about ten o'clock and the station was comfortably full. Except for three or four people, there was no concern whatever over the violence at hand. 'What is happening,' Mr. Cousins believes, 'is that the natural reactions of the individual against violence are being blunted. The individual is being desensitized by living history. He is developing new reflexes and new responses that tend to slow up the moral imagination and relieve him of essential indignation over impersonal hurt. He is becoming casual about brutality. He makes his adjustments to the commonplace, and nothing is more commonplace in our age than the ease with which life can be smashed or shattered. . . . There are some things we have no right ever to get used to. One of these most certainly is brutality. The other is the irrational. Both brutality and the irrational have now come together and are moving toward a dominant pattern. If the pattern is to be resisted and changed, a special effort must be made. A very special effort.' It must be made by those whose hearts are young.

So we make ideas live—by having them to start with, by relating them to our common humanity over all time, by preserving them from mediocrity and mechanization, by relating them morally to practical affairs. All this is well. But there is one thing more. They must receive the quickening touch of high imagination, that high imagination which is the crown of both learning and life. It arises whenever we are vitally aware of the full dimension of our existence, when our eyes and minds are really open to all expressions of greatness man has managed. It is maintaining what John Stuart Mill, whose *Essay on Liberty* is having its hundredth anniversary right now, once called 'a due balance among the faculties.' You remember how Mill escaped from an arid and desperate period in his own life by reading the poety of William Wordsworth. 'I seemed to draw,' he said, 'from a source of inward joy, of sympathetic and imaginative pleasure which could be shared in by all human beings. . . . It is the artist alone in whose hand Truth becomes impressive and a living principle of action.'

This high imagination, which moves us very near the green

altar of our human quest, includes our religious faith. This point I shall not labor. But here or somewhere every thoughtful soul encounters the Christian faith and its startling assertion—that we can realistically know the good and evil, the full terror and the full glory of the world, and yet believe in a responsible selfhood enhanced by mercy and infinite love, and a quality of life that carries within itself its long victory over death. Little wonder it takes some men and women a long time to weigh this amazing proposition. A faith like this can be reasonable, but it rests not on some logical postulate nor on some evidence our tiny hands can gather. It rests not even on the human heart and the nature of man. It rests on the nature of God and on a blazing Event in time, where an Idea lives in a Person. This is the kind of faith the actor in Archibald MacLeish's *J. B.* hints at when he says:

> It's God the Father I play—not
> God the boiling point of water!

This is the faith that restores the sundered shreds of our common life in 'the healing ministry of the Incarnation.' It is a faith beyond rumor and speculation. It flatly affirms, 'I know whom I have believed, and am persuaded that He is able to keep that which I have committed unto Him against that day.'

'To what green altar, O mysterious priest?' 'I am the vine and my Father is the husbandman. . . . I am the vine and ye are the branches.' In Greece or Palestine or Wooster, wherever men have lived, they have had persistent yearning for the green edge of a growing life. The worldly hopes they set their hearts upon cannot somehow cancel their aspiring souls. And thus plain men, men like you and me, would like, before they die, to bring at least one not unworthy gift to the altars that stir their imagination. Little wonder, as they sit within the stones of tall cathedrals and think of a living God and a risen Lord, that they are somehow reminded of the forests and the green places of the earth.

For the great Gothic cathedral of the thirteenth century grew up, as Sir James Yoxall wrote long ago, 'from the soil like a tree—

like a banyan, like a copse, like a forest of foliage; see how it flames at sunset, see how it flowers at dawn. . . . Silence, immensity, splendor, mute worship by the soul. Within the thousand gleams of gules and sapphire and orange-tawny at York let us kneel, and hear the young cherubic voices go soaring through the mist of light in the vault: "It doth not yet appear what we shall be!" Or within the amber gloom at Bourges let us bow the head, as we hear the deep chant, "*Te, lucis ante terminum*—To Thee, before the last light fades, Creator of all things, we pray!" '

# The Time of Beholding
## (1960)

We welcome to this baccalaureate morning the families and friends of the class of 1960. From all over the world they have come—these folks who only a few short years ago were little apple-eating animals making crayon marks on paper in the rationed years of World War II. Now they stand in the full sophistication of those who have jumped all the hurdles set in their way. If you have found your sons and daughters looking a little tired, do not blame it all on the higher learning in America. Other things go on here. The late Robert Benchley used to say, 'A great many people have come up to me and asked me how I manage to get so much work done and still keep looking so dissipated. My answer is, "Don't you wish you knew?" ' The secret, he went on to say, was a simple one, based on a well-known psychological principle. 'Anyone can do any amount of work, provided it isn't the work he is supposed to be doing at that moment.' Even so, there has been solid accomplishment here, and many a battle won. Frankly, we are very proud of your sons and daughters, and glad to have the chance to thank you for them.

They were born just as the world was preparing for World War II, with vast threats to freedom everywhere. It was the world of Munich, Manchuria, Barcelona, and the Sudetenland— of mad and cruel men proclaiming the new dispensation. The

Fuehrer, the dictator, was to relieve the common man of the burden of free will. The voice of Herman Goering echoed the sterile refrain of all the growing stooges of his time, 'My conscience is Adolf Hitler.' And soon it was the world of Poland and Holland and Belgium and France and the roll of the quick-crushing armies —of the few brave souls who rose into the red air over London and did so much for so many. And then it was Guadalcanal, Iwo Jima, and Okinawa, and the many who died everywhere, over the lands and the seven seas. So that now a man or a woman of twenty-one or twenty-two can still affirm man's free spirit under law, can reaffirm the moral order, tight though things now be.

And when they were barely started to school, and learning how not to spell, a brand-new world came riding on a white cloud dropping its fearful rain. The little geography books went shut and man's world became one—except that it didn't. We settled into pondering the ambiguous threats of our time: the atomic problem and the problem of overpopulation, seeking to steer our ironic way between the Scylla and Charybdis of whether we shall be either too many or too few.

Meantime, as if to distract us, there opens a whole new universe of rockets and telescopes and satellites and dizzying chase around the planets and the stars. We see deeper into the vast canyons of the sea, into the heart of whatever matter is. With new computers and electronic brains we attack problems and mysteries into which we now dare to think our way because for the first time we have a chance to manage the needed data. It is a world, we are told, in which 90 per cent of all the scientists who ever lived are still living, and where, one supposes, more than 90 per cent of the great moralists and poets and artists are long dead.

Oh, the class of 1960 have had a lot to look at. And in a few short years they will see much more—wonders and glories and incredible beauty; and terrors and ugliness to bow the head and break the heart. They will see 'elder truths, sad truths, grand truths, fearful truths.' For there will be a lot of these between now and the year of their fiftieth reunion, the year 2010. There will be a lot of time for beholding.

And this is the great thing: within this cosmic framework each solitary soul will have the high privilege of seeing it all through one man's eyes—his own. He is the jury and the judge, to whom 'all the arguments are addressed,' with whom 'all inquiry, knowledge, and vision begin and end.' Each man in his time has his chance to know whatever truth he will know in his lifetime, and to take his stand on that. For this is man's singular distinction—that he is not the passive, imperceipient spectator of what time drags before his eyes between birth and death. He half creates the very world he perceives. His eyes are informed eyes. He confers a meaning on life—out of his brain, his knowledge, his conscience, and all else that is in him. This is man's high and more-than-mortal privilege—that he does something to the world that tries to do something to him. He sees, not just things, but through things to whatever center of reality he is permitted to see. And when he does his best—probably more than once and on a variety of occasions—these are for him the times of beholding.

> The eye sinks inward, and the heart lies plain,
> And what we mean, we say, and what we would, we know.
> A man becomes aware of his life's flow. . . .
>
> And there arrives a lull in the hot race
> Wherein he doth forever chase
> That flying and elusive shadow, rest.
> An air of coolness plays upon his face
> And an unwonted calm pervades his breast.
> And then he thinks he knows
> The hills where his life rose,
> And the sea where it goes.
>
> (Matthew Arnold, "The Buried Life")

'God screens us evermore,' said Emerson, 'from premature ideas. . . . We cannot see things that stare us in the face, until the hour arrives when the mind is ripened; then we behold them, and the time when we saw them not is like a dream.'

For such hours of insight education should surely prepare a man. The passion to see things as they are, and not as they half-are, the capacity to weigh, compare, and evaluate; the scientific method; the imagination enriched by art, music, and literature; the desire to attain the high fidelities of everything; the perspective and awareness born of history and social studies; the insights of philosophy and religion—these are the obvious instruments for helping us to see into the life of things.

But my purpose this morning is not to extol the virtues of liberal study. I wish, rather, to suggest to those who already, I believe, have the tools for high insight, what some of the rules may be for anyone just now who hopes to come nearer to the truth, who hopes to be ready for the times of beholding that his own life will present to him.

The first suggestion is this: we must look outward and not just inward if we wish to see. To say this is not to disparage, of course, the high value of meditation and reflection, or even the work of the trained analyst. The quest for some order and quiet at the center of our being is a proper quest. From the heart are the issues of life. But this legitimate and necessary inwardness is a far different thing from the self-conscious and corrosive depth-hunting, the prideful massaging of our souls, a sentimental and glandular brooding over our own insides. (This reminds us too much of the embarrassed farmer who, according to legend, swallowed an egg whole by mistake; and he did not know whether to move and run the risk of breaking it or sit still and run the risk of hatching it.) Alfred Kazin last week, as *Time* magazine reported him, paid his respects to the current 'image of man' in the Broadway theater. 'It is concerned largely with "psychological man," the man who looks at nothing but himself, his own emotional wants, his own sexual satisfactions, none of which is now news to any of us and may for once, please God, be boring to other people. . . . I went to the theater to discover another world, the true world of imagination. . . . And the fuel of imagination, right now, can only be an enlarged voice of our human possibilities, and a smaller one for our tiresome little sins.'

To move outward, into the wonder of the natural world, into high deeds and selfless purpose, into the tangible and rich traditions of mankind, into beauty and excellence and the quest of some wisdom beyond any of our own—this is to gain sights and truths beyond ourselves. This is to prepare ourselves for the time of beholding. This puts us in the way of great things.

To put oneself in the way of understanding and the authentic news of what life is about, we must do a second thing. We must fight against the dehumanization of life itself. Not just against violence and the notion that human beings are expendable, but against all that mechanizes the spirit of man. Against seeing people as graphs and charts and statistics; against that great contemporary anesthesia, the Law of Averages. Against all attempts to manipulate us. 'Are we not all more or less,' asks Lewis Mumford, 'in the plight of that pathetic Marine colonel who, to explain his submission to his Communist inquisitors, said in so many words that the effect of their methods was just like that of American advertising: namely, to deprive him of choice.'

The times of beholding belong, not to robots, but to live and breathing men and women who do know what choice is and are willing to take some of the high creative risks. I do not mean recklessness or endorse Samuel Butler's wry comment that 'all progress is based upon a universal innate desire on the part of every organism to live beyond its income.' But I do believe that very early in life there come moments when a man has to choose between a smug security and high adventure. In that hour of critical choice comes one of the times of beholding.

Some of my colleagues will remember my delight in what the traveler often encounters out West—perhaps with fence or field for background—the stuffed or cardboard representation of a bucking bronco. This painted imitation beast is always a fearsome-looking thing, a rearing, untamed son of thunder. The pale tourist from the East, for a proper fee, can be photographed in chaps, spurs, and brightly colored cowboy shirt, triumphantly subduing this wild animal. By such innocent deception a Casper Milquetoast becomes for a shining moment the Lone Ranger's brother, and sends the postcard to the folks back home.

It is a haunting symbol—this imitation rider on the imitation horse: making all the safe motions and going nowhere. Wherever the vital spark has died, wherever men seek a low security above all else, wherever men stand with faded marching orders in their hands, they have kinship with the lifeless horse and the lifeless rider. It is hard to understand this spirit of tiny calculation when one thinks of all the frontiers that open now—where the grand views await the time of beholding; vistas undreamed of twenty years ago.

There is another hour of encounter, another time of beholding, even for those who keep their humanity alive, who do good things in the world, and choose the road of high adventure. And this is the principal hour—when a man decides who he is, really means it, and knows that what he sees and determines will affect the rest of his life. This comes in various moments, sometimes in crises, sometimes in quieter hours and ways. But the question is always the same—Who am I? An animal in quick transit between birth and death in a blind universe that has no meaning, awareness, and direction? Or a living soul with the mark of the eternal world upon him?

For a great many reasons I have no wish this morning to discuss the grounds for belief in immortality. At the fag end of four college years the class of 1960 has no desire to hear the President of the College try to tidy up in the last few minutes all the high matters of the soul. What I wish rather to assert is that any attempt to evade the question of whether the life of a given human being is temporary or eternal is a defection of intelligence. All noble stoicism to the contrary, it makes an enormous difference what a person believes on this score. A conviction that his life has eternal significance is bound to affect all a man is and does—his actions, his loyalties, his daily sense of himself and other men. Any ignoring of this question is not, as I say, a failure of religion. It is a failure of our wits. The hour when we come to some estimate of this matter is, in very truth, the time of beholding.

One thing is quite clear. The Christian Church did not leave the question of eternal life a matter of wishful thinking and philosophical inquiry. For it sees the living God not as something vague and convenient that you can use to open the Senate with prayer or lay a cornerstone or stamp on a coin. He is not something with which you can play hide-and-seek, pray to as the preface to an address by an eminent biologist proving He does not exist and then offer a benediction—to whom, one wonders. A Communist dictator can hardly with straight face rule Him out of the universe and then call on Him to witness that 'my hands are clean and my soul is pure.' The time of beholding is not the time of seeing double.

The Christian faith, as Arnold Lunn reminds us, does not dilute John 3:16 to read: 'God so loved the world that He inspired a certain Jew to inform his contemporaries that there was a great deal to be said for loving one's neighbor.' If Jesus had been merely a great man or discerning philosopher we would never have had the Church that bears His name. The Church arises out of an Event in history, a shattering revelation. And what the Church declares is that God was in Christ reconciling the world to Himself—within a context of eternal life.

If I could wish anything for a young man or woman this morning it would be the wish that, early in his days and far ahead of some desperate need, he could come to feel that his own life had eternal meaning. Tolstoy used to complain that we had so lost the power to turn our minds to bear on these important things that only the near thought of death could bring us to the sense of them. This seems a pity if it be so. It means missing so much now

—this side of the hospital corridor. So much of ardor, so much of joy, so much of beholding.

It would have been almost impossible to take a text for these remarks this morning. The word 'behold' runs some three hundred times through the Old and the New Testament. Sometimes it is the trumpet prelude to some high announcement. Sometimes it is in a much lower key, as a kind of reminder to pay attention to the narrative, much as if somebody were being punched awake in church. We are told to look at a great many things—the rising herbs and trees of Eden, a man just given the knowledge of good and evil, the visions of the prophets, the fig tree withered away, the lepers, the sick and the lame, the bridegroom coming, the beam in our own eye, the house that is left unto us desolate. And, besides these, the Lamb of God taking away the sins of the world, and the Tabernacle of God with man. And in the Revelation, that masterpiece of beholding—the white cloud, the horses, and the dragons. A quiet figure saying, 'Behold, I stand at the door and knock.' And 'Behold, I make all things new!'

One winter afternoon in 1924 I went to Cleveland to see Bernard Shaw's *St. Joan*. It was one of the memorable days of my life. An English chaplain, out of a fanatic love of his own island and therefore a hatred of all things French, demands of the Earl of Warwick that Joan of Arc be put to death with certain haste. On the day of the execution in the marketplace at Rouen, the chaplain is on hand to watch the burning. He later staggers in from the courtyard as if he were demented, a broken man, his face streaming with tears. The Earl of Warwick, calm and imperturbable, tries to comfort him: 'If you have not the nerve to see these things, why do you not do as I do, and stay away?'

'You don't know: you haven't seen: it is so easy to talk when you don't know. . . . But when it is brought home to you; when you see the thing. . . .'

In the famous epilogue of the play it is years later. The chaplain is seen as a touched but tender old man: 'I tell my folks they must be very careful. I say to them, "If you only saw what you think about you would think quite differently about it. . . . You see, I did a very cruel thing once because I did not know what cruelty was like. I had not seen it, you know. That is the great thing: you must see it. And then you are redeemed and saved." '

Another voice asks, 'Must then a Christ perish in torment in every age to save those that have no imagination?'

And Joan wonders at the close, 'O God that madest this beautiful earth, when will it be ready to receive Thy saints? How long, O Lord, how long?'

# The Other Languages
## (1962)

Some years ago, so the story runs, a society woman who collected celebrities gave a large dinner. The guests of honor were the late Oliver Herford, one of our droller citizens, and a famous military man. At the end of the meal, the lady rose and beamed, without previous warning, 'Mr. Herford will now improvise a poem in honor of the hostess.' Herford sank down into his chair. 'Oh, no,' he muttered. 'Have the General fire a cannon.' Your sons and daughters deserve a louder salute than can probably be fired by a college officer, as weary as they are from the winter chores, the nightly reconstruction of brick walks, and the general ardors of learning and Presbyterianism. What we can do is explore one theme that I believe has meaning and importance.

And our theme is this: that beyond what we regard as language itself—the words and phrases and sentences, native or foreign, that form our concepts and, except for the mathematicians, express most of what we think we know—beyond these are the other languages, the wordless truths, that speak to us powerfully. They teach and move us, and through them we become much of whatever we do become. Our estimate of life, must, or should, take account of what they say. Moreover, they address our whole being and not some fragmented part of us. They speak to thought and will and feeling—to all that we are. And my baccalaureate wish for those who aspire to be liberally educated men and women is that these other languages may have a large place in their lives forever.

To say this is not to deny logic and reason and verbal exactitude. Indeed, I share the concern that our verbal culture, through the decline of the linguistic disciplines and the fierce competition of our well-known mass media, may lag behind as the weakest part of our whole cultural heritage. Notice, morever, that it is only by words that I can convey the idea of the other languages at all. This has its embarrassment. One remembers Dr. Johnson's horse-sense about people who cannot find words to describe what they have experienced. He once said of a certain metaphysical poet, that if Mr. X had experienced the unutterable, he would be well advised not to utter it.

If I ask you to think this morning about these so-called other languages—the great communications that lie beyond language itself—I, logically, have no words with which to express these things. I can only point and suggest what they are. I cannot convey their reality. Only you can give them life and make them real, out of your own experience. It is you who must from this point help give this baccalaureate address—and I ask your help. I believe that these other languages have spoken and do speak to us all. They are familiar and real and important. They are a crucial part of what life will be for us or what we shall conclude life is. May God help the education that neglects them.

We begin with the obvious other languages—with music and painting and sculpture and architecture. Are these not so? Are they merely diversion and agreeable experience, or are they revelation? If I asked you to give your own account of the world, what part would they have in your philosophy? Not everyone would give them place. Dean Stanley of Westminster Abbey confessed once that the only music he really liked was a drum solo. But to most of us the high arts seem like 'the breath and finer spirit of all knowledge.' This very fact tells us much about the arts—and even more about ourselves. To be sure, the B-Minor Mass, the Sistine Chapel, the Winged Victory, Chartres Cathedral, the 'Madonna of the Rocks'—or, for that matter, the small deep-set windows of Le Corbusier's chapel at Ronchamp—cannot logically prove the nature of reality to a philosopher. But the philosopher dare not leave them out of his own account. To deny these things their place in our total being—in our estimate of God or man—would make us as ridiculous as the fellow who went round complaining that his lint suit was always picking up little pieces of blue serge.

This winter I have been reading a hard and closely reasoned book that makes you earn every step of the way and any view you gain of an intelligent, divine universe. At the same time I was trying to memorize the music of the *Te Deum* of Verdi, the glorious performance of which was the event of our early spring. If now, suddenly, you ask me, 'What is the world like?,' I would confess I should have to take far more account of the 'other language' of the *Te Deum*'s music—the things 'that broke through language and escaped'—than I would of the hard and highly rewarding book.

For there are moments beyond language where deep answers unto deep and we feel the living presence of a power not ourselves. We feel what Denis de Rougemont wrote of those efforts which he calls 'the exercise of the whole being of man' in an effort to 'coincide better with the order of Creation, to love it better, and to re-establish ourselves in it.' It is our 'invocation to the lost harmony,' like a prayer 'corresponding to the second petition of the Lord's Prayer—"Thy Kingdom Come."'

We are vastly occupied these days with the subconscious. Yet 'very few of us,' as Gilbert Highet says, 'realize that the subconscious has to be fed regularly, has to be supplied with material to nourish it.' This material can be religion and the arts or the 'meager substitutes' we are daily offered. And the great materials that form even our subconscious mind, outrunning language as we commonly know it, do 'say something about the world'—and about us. They are 'not only decorations; they are messages.'

All the great symbols contribute to the truth of our particular world. The massive power of these symbols—be they the swastika or the cross—is that they become another language. Their genius, as Thomas Carlyle saw long ago, lies in their combination of speech plus silence, which leaves the infinite to the imagination. Indeed, silence itself, in our 'twittering world' is a kind of other language. 'It delivers thy tongue for one day; on the morrow, how much clearer are thy purposes and duties; what wreck and rubbish have those mute workmen within thee swept away, when intrusive noises were shut out!' We are so made that even silence is another language.

So, of course, is the natural world around us. It is one of the prime relationships we have, speaking its own language in a thousand forms to every generation. What treasures of memory would we have this morning if each person here could summon all at once the places and sounds and sights his mind has stored away—the grandeur of seas and deserts and mountains and waterfall, the filtering light in a dark forest, the turn of a summer road, the sudden song or flower, the rising of the winter moon, the lapping of water by some quiet shore; dawn and sunset and night with its stars. All these 'how old to tell of, how new to see.' 'Day unto day uttereth speech, and night unto night showeth knowledge. There is no speech nor language where their voice is not heard.'

In the drama of our life, 'the earth itself,' writes H. M. Tomlinson, 'is the oldest of characters; it was here when the earliest of us arrived.' When you are properly reminded of it by some man who can really see and feel it, 'the shadow of Something which is greater than mortal life begins to fall upon your reading' . . . 'For a bare instant' you 'feel the riddle can be solved.' In many an hour has not this been your history and mine?

But modern man, Joseph Wood Krutch holds, ' "understands" more and more as he sees and hears less and less. By the time he

has reached high-school age he has been introduced to the paradox that the chair on which he sits is not the hard object it seems
to be but a collection of dancing molecules. He learns to deal, not
with objects, but with statistics, and before long he is introduced
to the idea that God is a mathematician, not the creator of things
seen, and heard, and felt. As he is taught to trust less and less the
evidence of the five senses with which he was born, he lives less
and less in the world which they seem to reveal.'

We tend to pull away from the prime things and their elemen-
tal voices. We forget how even materials and objects have a life
of their own and a language for one who can hear it—a man like
the late Charles Kettering. Some of you know my fondness for
Mr. Kettering's account of the day when the piston-action of a
Diesel engine he had improved was challenged by a professor
who said the action violated all the laws of engineering. 'But it is
working!' Mr. Kettering rejoined, 'how can you deny it?' 'Well,'
his visitor replied, 'I am a professor of engineering.' 'Yes,' said
Mr. Kettering, 'but have you ever been a piston?'

In a far more crucial way, we often smother reality beneath
our concepts and our abstractions. The great words like 'truth'
and 'liberty' and 'compassion'—how they wither and grow detached from the specific instances that lend them life. We stifle
our awareness and galvanize our hearts, we refrain from glorious
causes and fail to hate and love enough, because we have general-
ized and catalogued experience and cut ourselves off from the
agony, the terror, the suffering, the power, and the glory we
ought to feel. The result is endless compromise with injustice and
nonsense and violence, and man's inhumanity to man. Our ears and
eyes and hearts are stopped against the other language of real
things. We rationalize that we no longer actually know.

If the arts and nature and the prime realities of life have a special voice of their own, there is yet another language—the language of greatness itself. For the quality of greatness, be it in
small things or large, carries its own annunciation. It speaks from

actions and men's lives—the living and dead. It shines quite over and beyond the actual language of literature or the utterance of any man. It is the absence of it—the lack of any evident tact for the spirit's real life—that makes many a philosopher and theologian seem a mere rumor-monger and system-builder, alien to the very world he seeks to deliver.

You and I deeply want some encounter with the best there is. We feel a singular loneliness without it, and we rally to it as to the sound of a trumpet. Mr. Whitehead long ago reminded us that the habitual vision of greatness was what education should afford to men. I think we caught some glimpse of this vision here the other day in the presence of Robert Frost. Beyond any words in his poems or in his speech, there was the eloquent reality of the man himself and the far ranges he has traveled. This comes through. We have known it for years in the presence of Arthur Compton, and this presence is abiding. As George Bernard Shaw once said of William Morris, 'You can lose a man like that by your own death, but not by his.' The sheer reality of Abraham Lincoln spoke to men, in his own lifetime and now, quite beyond anything he did or said. 'There was a harmony in him,' Brooks Atkinson once wrote, 'tuned to something finer than anything I am aware of in this world.'

Mr. Atkinson, incidentally, elsewhere in his New York diary, *Once Around the Sun*, gives us a symbol of the voice of greatness: 'Above the clatter and rumble of the traffic in Times Square, the diapason of the *Queen Mary*'s bedlam—nervous, petty, sharp, impatient. But the voice of the *Queen Mary* is grand. The tone is deep and round; the volume is tremendous as it pours down the cacophonous canyons of the city. . . . When the *Queen Mary* is ready to go to sea she speaks plainly enough to be heard by thousands of landlocked citizens in New York and New Jersey.'

If you who are parents asked what graduation wish I could most make for your sons and daughters, I could tell you plainly.

My top wish would not be long life, or happiness, or worldly
goods and place, or even freedom from suffering and disappointment. This would be my top wish for anyone—that he clearly
know the difference between joy and satisfaction. Nothing else I
know so clears the head and heart, confers moral insight, or
renders life so rich.

Satisfaction is a wide-ranging word. Its root meaning is 'to do
or have enough,' which shows its very ambiguity. It has a termi-
nus. It may mean anything from the filling of basic needs and de-
sires, the freedom from repression we hear so much about, to the
pride one might feel in good work done, in some harmony of living rightly realized, in home or family. But joy is a pure thing
and, out of itself, can be endless. It is the white flame that lights
our whole being to new levels of insight and comprehension and
makes us creatures of more than mortal privilege.

Joy marks the difference between good and evil. It is the highest morality. One may find satisfaction of a sort in lust or gain or
shrewdness or greed. But he will not find joy. Joy is what
Spinoza called it—'man's passage to a greater perfection.' It can,
in many ways, be earned. But there is also something about it of
pure gift. When you and I discover it we may come upon it in
many ways—perhaps mostly through the power of some superior
affection, the love for some person or some friend, or the love of
God. 'Of all the worn, smudged, dog's-eared words in our vocab-
ulary,' says Aldous Huxley, whose own spiritual journey has
been a long one, ' "love" is surely the grubbiest, smelliest, slimi-
est. Bawled from a million pulpits, lasciviously crooned through
hundreds of millions of loud-speakers, it has become an outrage
to good taste and decent feeling, an obscenity which one hesitates
to pronounce. And yet it has to be pronounced, for after all, love
is the last word.' Dante said it moved the sun and the other stars.
And as one of our own time saw, with deepest insight, 'That end
of social man' is not just communication, with all the words flying back and forth, but 'communion in time through love, which
is beyond time.'

The joy I speak of is often the product of some thought realized in words. The mathematicians seem to know it often. It is
often the flower of honest work well done. But it has tremendous
help from the other languages we have thought about this
morning—from the arts, and music, and nature, and primal things
and greatness; when a man's fractured and disconnected life
moves into some kind of exhilarating wholeness when with

> an eye made quiet by the power
> Of harmony, and the deep power of joy,
> We see into the life of things.

This is when a man feels himself no longer a thing of shreds and
patches, some brief traveler between two oblivions—but as if he
were carrying some precious cup in his hand to the highest altars
of insight and desire in a journey that might last forever.

Ultimately, of course, a man cannot rejoice in anything except
the nature of things. His joy will measure the faith he holds. It
takes some persons a long time to know what that faith is. Once
found it can be the very heart of joy—and sorrow and loss and
tragedy have no dominion over it. This faith can have its ground
in reason. But here again the other languages begin to speak: 'In
the beginning was the Word, and the Word was with God, and
the Word was God.'

Listen, if you will, to the great language informed by the
'other languages,' the words of W. H. Auden's vision of the
Way, the Truth, the Life: *

> He is the Way.
> Follow Him through the Land of Unlikeness;
> You will see rare beasts,
>     and have unique adventures.

* From *The Collected Poetry of W. H. Auden,* copyright 1944 by W. H.
Auden. Reprinted by permission of Random House, Inc., and Faber and
Faber, Ltd.

He is the Truth.
Seek Him in the Kingdom of Anxiety;
You will come to a great city that has
    expected your return for years.

He is the Life.
Love Him in the World of the Flesh;
And at your marriage all its
    occasions shall dance with joy.

# To the Editorial Dimension
## (1963)

The oldest person I ever met was ten years old. I was six. After school each day he went by our house and carried under his arm his fourth-grade textbook, Frye's *First Steps in Geography*. It seemed to me an enormous book. On the cover were two huge circles showing both sides of the world and six continents. I looked on all this with awe. If I could ever live to be ten, make it into the fourth grade, and carry the world under one arm, all would be well. That would be the day.

All our lives somebody keeps going by the house that way. As the swift years pass, he carries a great variety of things—the first report card, the first ticket that takes us out of town, the first pay check, the first clear call to some duty, the first harsh glimpse of some new reality, first love, or the first dream. The news of birth goes with him, and the news of death; the news of children and the grandchildren. He bears the fragment of a new song, the text of a play, the line of a poem, or a painting that opens the eyes for the first time. He brings a first look into the nature of things, some vision of the state, the news of war and peace, or the hint of man's ideal life, which is 'his normal life as it might someday be.' Someone is always going by.

Tomorrow he brings diplomas under his arm. I know, because they are already signed and sealed. Not all the seniors have taken honors. Once Dean DeVane, of Yale College, asked an under-graduate, 'Are you in the upper half of your class?' The boy re-plied, 'No, sir, I'm in the half that makes the upper half possible.' Whatever half they represent, the diplomas tomorrow are evi-dence of a solid accomplishment. But diplomas tell simply what has happened. One day ahead of their delivery, I want this morn-ing to be an invitation—an invitation to what may still be.

I want the recurring passer-by I saw at six to go again before the door of our house. The document he bears this morning is not a big geography book, but the copy of a first-class newspaper. The paper has no date. The events it tells of are irrelevant. You may remember James Thurber's favorite newspaper man, John A. McNulty, who had his own Irish way of putting time and his-tory in their place. When once the talk turned gravely to the year 1885, McNulty said, 'That was the year the owls were so bad.' Thurber loved him, and it's easy to see why.

Our paper has no date. But it does have an editorial page. Let us assume it a first-class one, the kind that gives the paper a heart and soul. Let it be a synthesis, perhaps, of the great editors—the work of a Charles Dana, a James Gordon Bennett, Jr., a Horace Greeley, a William Allen White, or a Henry Watterson. In the very nature of that editorial page, if you read it well, you will find the summons to a certain quality of life to which all liberal studies invites you—a life that aspires to the editorial dimension.

This address began one morning several months ago in Wash-ington, D.C. This may, indeed, account for any confusion you detect in it. A group of men, mostly college presidents, was en-gaged for two days in a conference on liberal education. The second morning I awoke with what was for me a sudden and helpful conviction—that the real difference a liberal education can make, wherever and however you acquire it, in college or on your own, is the difference between receiving and recording the facts and the relating and interpreting of facts in the light of all the rest we know. It is the difference between data and significance. The reporter tells you what happened. The editor tells you what it means.

I would not, of course, disparage the good reporter. He, too, has his art and his powerful vocation. By virtue of what he sees, selects, and vividly presents, he is his own kind of editor. He does not have, however, the scope and freedom of the editorial page.

A good editorial page is surely the lively example of a liberal education. It glows like a warm fire with the significance of things. It draws on literature and history, on art and politics, on the natural sciences, on philosophy and religion. It gathers into relationship the miscellaneous events, the shreds and patches of our fragmented life. It keeps our heritage alive and reminds us of what we have forgotten—the 'things silently gone out of mind,' of 'things violently destroyed.' It gives form to experience. It suggests what we should value and honor and love. And, in the dark and desperate hour, it rallies men to greatness. The editor is a 'man for all seasons.' This is his work, the height and the depth of it, and this is the 'editorial dimension.'

I speak of this today, not to furnish a treatise on liberal study, but to invite the senior class to a certain kind of life, long after college. For the education they have known is not merely the open door to some business or profession, or some adornment it is nice to have. Liberal study is designed to furnish a man against the hundred erosions of his mind and heart the years try to give him—against the day he does not read enough, think enough, and feel enough, the day when his very spirit cries out, 'Where is wisdom to be found? And where is the place of understanding?' Then it is he needs to be reminded that men can read and think and feel and comprehend, that they can have, if they really want it, an adequately human life—that they can aspire, humbly and sincerely, to the editorial dimension.

The great editors have had four outstanding qualities. And the first we have already suggested—their search for leading principles and a broad view of man's role as man. Years ago, when the threat was less, George Santayana complained that never before had men known so many facts and been master of so few principles. In her fine inaugural address, President Rosemary Park, of Barnard, paid just homage to the specialists on whom society depends in our time of expanding knowledge, but cited them also as a present danger. She held they must be 'continually confronted' by 'the lay person,' who, seeking 'a richer and more creative truth than the truth of particular discovery' will 'challenge the specialist for the public good.'

I have mentioned James Thurber before. Perhaps you remember his satire on the opthalmologist and the psychologist, 'each of them concerned only with his own end of the optic nerve, which happens to join the eyeball and the brain.' When a certain patient began seeing double, the psychiatrist thought the problem was the man's inability to decide 'which one of two girls he was in love with.' The eye-man cured the condition with certain drops. Listen also to this voice from out a hundred years ago: 'If we have been accustomed to deplore the spectacle, among the artisan class, of a workman occupied during his whole life in nothing but making knife handles or pin heads, we may find something quite as lamentable in the intellectual class, in the exclusive employment of the human brain in resolving equations or classifying insects. The moral effect is, unhappily, analogous in the two cases. It occasions a miserable indifference about the general course of human affairs as long as there are equations to resolve and pins to manufacture.' Indeed, the future version of 'The Man with the Hoe' may not be Millet's moving portrait of the French peasants bent by toil, 'the emptiness of ages in his face,' but that of the scholar and researcher grubbing away at only his own row, cut off from himself and the society of men. It is quite wrong, of course, to make the specialist a whipping boy. We need his service and his precise knowledge and discovery. But it is fair to hope with Hans Zinsser, the bacteriologist, that 'one type of intelligent occupation should increase capacity for comprehension in general.'

The pressures on us are enormous. The other night I went down Fifth Avenue and saw the spires of St. Patrick's Cathedral rising against the lighted sky. They spoke of eternity. But just beyond them, in almost comic contrast, the electric sign of *Newsweek*'s tall building reminded us it was precisely 7:05 p.m. on a day fast moving to its close. Increasingly and understandingly, we live in this double world of the immediate and the timeless, the new knowledge and the ancient wisdom. And, because we are human, living in just one of them will not do. It makes us smaller than we are. Men who think at all cannot settle very long for their own bench or work desk, an occasional day at the beach, or for any form of tranquilized mediocrity. We have a built-in yearning for wholeness—for the meaning of our discoveries, for the totality of the world into which we were born. We yearn for the editorial dimension.

The second mark of the good editors is this—they have causes and commitments. They fight many a good fight—and not just by fits and starts and gestures. They are not like the first Augustus, who 'once a year dressed like a mendicant, and sitting at his palace gate, held out an imperial hand for a beggar's alms.' The good editors have fought poverty, disease, and corruption day after day. And so doing, they furnish a direction for us all. The academic world rightly reaches suspension of judgment till all the facts are in. But it gives no man a license to practice a perpetual neutrality. Some things have been right and some things wrong from the beginning of the world. No amount of learning exonerates us from trying at least to come down on the right side. Ideas are one thing, and the will is another. No man among us has cared more for ideas and nice discriminations than Lionel Trilling. But Mr. Trilling does not say our direct need is more information or even more intelligence. 'Surely,' he says, 'the great work of our time is the restoration and the reconstitution of the will.' To say this is to move toward the editorial dimension.

There is a third quality of a good editor. He cares about the home ground. He must occupy himself with national and international affairs. But, first of all, he is a citizen of his own town and community. Thus he is a shining rebuke to those whose hearts can bleed easily, as they ought to bleed, for somebody in Indonesia or Alabama, but who lack the compassion or the moral courage to take a strong stand for something on the home ground. Even the town of Wooster has not fully earned the right to disparage Alabama.

In a society where 20 per cent of our American people move their homes every year, where local roots go down less and less, it is agreeable to think of men like Henry Watterson, working out from Louisville, Nat Howard and Louis Seltzer from Cleveland, and, if I may say so, the editor of our own home town. Tomorrow we shall be honoring one who, at the age of ninety, is still active every day as a citizen-editor in Oklahoma City, which has been his passionate concern for years, while at the same time he opened windows to the world.

In 1895, William Allen White became the editor of the *Emporia Gazette*. At his death in 1944, he had a service of nearly fifty years. When other more ambitious men were looking nervously about them for the next main chance, William Allen White pegged himself down to stay. He hoped always to sign 'from Emporia' after his name. He refused all offers that came from the great dailies. The *Tribune* tried to land him in Chicago. Joseph Pulitzer begged him to come to New York and join the *World*. He always said 'no.' Why leave 'tree-lined Emporia?'

Somebody once asked Mozart for whom he had composed *The Magic Flute*—probably meaning for what Prince or Cardinal. Mozart answered, 'I wrote *The Magic Flute* for myself and three friends.' Not just out of the heart, but out of the ground where you stand, are the issues of life. One of the great dimensions is to go down where you are. My dearest wish for some member of the senior class is that he may live in one place all his life. He may, if he does so, be guilty of an un-American activity. But there will be compensations.

The great editors have had not just a concern for principles, for causes, and for the home ground. They have a fourth distinction. They have an enduring hope. Realists by the very nature of their profession, familiar with 'all living, both the dark and bright,' they nevertheless contend for realizable human goals, for the ultimate victory of truth and decency, for the peaceable kingdom that can come. They give nerve and heart to their fellow men. 'Is there somewhere, in the stuff that holds humanity together,' asks William Allen White, 'some force, some conservation of spiritual energy, that saves the core of every noble hope?'

My word to this class comes to its head in a plea for that kind of hope. I can wish its members something better than a poor slavery to the stale clichés that banish hope and desecrate our time—the easy notion that machines will swallow us, that some sacred law of averages can unerringly predict our future, that reason is a delusion, character an amiable myth, and the will but water; that, in a world already doomed to its own self-dismissal, we stand, like Scott Fitzgerald's man, 'at twilight on a deserted range, with an empty rifle in my hands and the targets down.' I could wish them something better than the sleazy moral relativism that rapidly grows about us. I could wish them a hopeful belief in standards. The anthropologists have rightly reminded us that some values are relative to specific cultures. But that's not the whole truth. Clyde Kluckhohn, one of the best anthropologists of our time, reminded us: 'Most of the writers and thinkers whom the judgment of humanity has called "great" have come to the conclusion that men are influenced in their behavior by transcendental standards and these standards are by no means completely culture-bound but have elements of universality.'

We do have the right to believe in and to work for some prevailing order, for some common law that can supply the basis for
a peaceful world. And our only persistence is

> to hope till hope creates
> From its own wreck the thing it contemplates.

Another hope is demanded of us—that we have hope of other
men and women, who are deeper than their looks, their actions,
and their failures. They outrun the catalogues made of them.
Thoreau at Walden could have been written off as a country
hick. He was not that. Jefferson at Monticello could have been a
Virginia snob. He wasn't. Abraham Lincoln could have been the
no-good son of a no-good father. He wasn't. Keats and Shakespeare, someone pointed out, sound like two of the ugliest possible names. But they are names of glory. To fail to seek the depth
in other men is hope's own violation. If we do not search and
hope for this in others, and persist in trying to find it, how dare
we look at ourselves? Emerson told us that all his life he was en-
deavoring to teach one doctrine—'the infinitude of the private
man.' This we can believe in, perversely if need be. The day we
close the book on other men, we close it on ourselves. For, if we
love not men whom we have seen, how can we love God whom
we have not seen? It is as plain as that.

Frankly, I would not know how to speak of hope in this way
apart from the Christian faith. The reporter's account of life, if
he took only a quick look at the common man, would run something like this: birth, something very mixed, and death. But there
was One life that went far beyond this. He was a brand-new dimension. As a result, He went everywhere and passed into history, art, music, literature, and all intellectual inquiry—and into
the lives of millions of men living and dead. Think of what He
had become in the life of the gracious, lovable, humble man who
died last week at the Vatican, John XXIII. If you are a thoughtful person, if you want things to mean something, if you take life
out into the editorial dimension, you'll have trouble avoiding

Jesus Christ. One who was not able to avoid Him, one to whom He came as blazing light, witnessed to Him everywhere he could go in the ancient world. He thought of Him in great dimensional terms—that we are all members of one body,

> For [he said] I am persuaded, that neither death, nor life, nor angels, nor principalities, nor powers, nor things present, nor things to come,
> Nor height, nor depth, nor any other creature, shall be able to separate us from the love of God, which is in Christ Jesus, our Lord.

# The Fifth Year
## (1965)

Oscar Wilde once said, 'Whenever people talk to me about the weather, I always feel certain that they mean something else.' I had a similar conviction not long ago when somebody asked me, 'What are the ground rules for a baccalaureate address?' I didn't know any. But I was suddenly very sure there ought to be some. And the first one is, for the speaker, 'Realize that not all you say will be heard.' For at least the fathers here this morning will be almost entirely preoccupied with wondering how the accumulation of four college years can be packed into one small car.

The second rule is, 'Don't try to cover the universe in one short morning.' The faculty have had their more extended try at this, and even they have left a lot uncovered. Friends used to say of a man of boundless energy they all admired, 'His only trouble is that he thinks God intends to do all He has in mind while he's still living.' No baccalaureate should try to exhaust the divine purpose.

The third rule for a baccalaureate is to try to suggest a few things of interest or use in the hope that at least one may, in retrospect, be remembered.

The fourth rule is obligatory: 'Somehow manage to say, before you quit, the best thing you know, the thing on which you would willingly bet your life. Even if what you say is wrong, the occasion demands this kind of sincerity. To this point you ought to come.'

Actually, our theme this morning is a homely one, related though it be to the shining Scripture you have just heard read. It begins with something very near at hand. Time after time I have heard seniors wistfully remark, 'If only I had a fifth year!' They would then, one gathers, take all the courses they have not had time to take. They would think about all they have not had time to think about. One gets the general impression that, given one more year, they would put the Renaissance to shame. Indeed, I heard all this, almost in such words, only a week ago.

The literal wish for a fifth year is, of course, quite insincere. I suggested to one student longing for it, that a fifth year could very easily be arranged. He could be flunked into it. He ran for cover like a stricken deer. Nevertheless, the feeling, the haunting desire for this added time, for the year that would enrich us—that feeling is exactly right. It honors anyone who has it.

For this fifth year—which is but a way of saying 'the rest of our lives'—is the whole point of a college and the objective of any education worth the name. Wooster's program, indeed, rests solidly on the assumption that a college graduate is not an educated man. He is a potentially educated one, who knows how to continue his education all the rest of his days. The very term 'graduation' suggests, to be sure, something of this sort—a life of renewal after renewal in the unfolding wonder of a world the mind can discover and possess. For we are all in the fifth year, we who are much past twenty. And we can be in it with all our mind and heart and soul, warm and alive—with curiosity and awareness and sensitivity to a world 'forever young and still to be enjoyed.' And so on, given reasonable health and blessing, to the day of our death.

Solon, the Greek, wrote, 'I grow old always learning many new things.' When he was traveling once in Egypt a venerable priest said to him, 'O Solon! Solon! you Greeks are always children. There isn't an old man among you.'

A variety of things will enrich the fifth year. Graduate or professional school, the first job, marriage, children, birth and death, joy and sorrow, the whole human comedy and tragedy; travel and communication; a world that can now quite literally be in anybody's heart as it has never been in the heart of any preceding generation; new things in space and in the depths of the sea—a look beyond the two billion light years; the instruments with which to think about matters we could not think about or more than guess at before; a recovery of the past as men have never before recovered it; a new face to the far horizons as we stand on the shoulders of giants taller than men have ever stood upon before. The fifth year opens out endlessly.

But it will not be all velvet. Those who tomorrow morning begin their fifth year will not necessarily have it all made to order. The old ghosts will still rattle through the house of life, and things will still go 'boomp' in the frequent dark. Some of these apparitions they will inherit. Some they will create for themselves, knowing full well the bitter truth that

> Whatever flares upon the night
> Man's own resinous heart has fed.

Out of this looming variety, I would name five things, with uneven time for each, that in the new fifth year will be important to the class of 1965, and to us all. I shall put these in the form of wishes—for them and for us all.

And the first wish for the fifth year is a new belief in man, in what is fully human. George Orwell's world of 1984, when men will have lost their souls to the machines, is but nineteen years away. And I for one am not scared, despite the fact that even now in the administration building the only room favored with air-conditioning is the one that houses the computer. The rest of us can suffer as we will. But you can always talk back to a computer. You can make it blush or at least flash an embarrassed red light. These are the questions Joseph Wood Krutch, that enlightened and stalwart humanist, would put to a machine: Can it have children? Does it have any ideas about itself? Does it 'believe' the mechanistic theories of life are true? Can it sympathize with anybody? Can it be happy or miserable? Does it ever, by some unaccustomed flickering in its tubes, show that it considers something amusing? Does it prefer one thing to another?

No, man is much too wonderfully obstinate to be subdued by the big machines, the big cities, or the other big conspiracies against his nature. He will not be caught 'shrinking into a statistic.' Even in New York and Chicago, Irwin Edman once reminded us, there is solitude among the crowds. 'One need not follow Thoreau into the wilderness to practice his isolation, nor Buddha into the desert to achieve his meditation.' The mind and the soul fight back against the brass invaders. Indeed, my own last-ditch faith in the struggle against a computer-dominated world is in the Presbyterians. They will never go along with any one thing that far.

If man loses his own humanity it will not be that the machines have got him. It will be that something important has dropped out of his mind and heart, that he has emasculated the definition of himself. It is this high definition that all decent education strives to keep alive. The Freudian death-wish, I heard Bryant Kirkland recently say, is not literally the wish to die or commit suicide. It is the wish to become a thing instead of a person—to avoid the choices persons have to make, the joys and sorrows of a love really given or refused, the sacrifices really made, the high risks taken. It wishes nothing of the hard-won wisdom of the lady, married forty-seven years and the mother of six children, who said very simply, 'Love is what you've been through with somebody.'

And if we have this strong belief in man and in what is human, we are strangely insincere if this belief does not create in us a new and practical care for man. As Arnold Toynbee and others have told us, for the first time in history we know that we now have the means of giving to every living person in the world the chance to make for himself a decent human life. This is the haunting, demanding news we now know. After such knowledge what forgiveness? The very advance of our powers and possibilities calls for a new belief in man.

This leads us straightway to our second wish—a new belief in courage. I mean the vast variety of courage short of war. It was in a fight, of course, that Winston Churchill insisted that courage was the highest of all the qualities because it guaranteed all the others. This be as it may, there is still, in the peaceful tasks of mankind, in the work still to do, a perpetual invitation to courage —to the whole range of what William James called the moral equivalent of war. More than ever we need the courage to go against, if need be, the prevailing mode, the courage to back, in reflective commitment, 'the lost causes, the forsaken beliefs, the impossible loyalties.'

The aim of education is to produce good minds, but not spineless intellectuals. Time and again in history, as in the Germany of Hitler, we have seen the uncommitted intellect surrender to the first committed brute that came along. John Foster Dulles used to remark that his experience in international affairs had impressed him with two things—the small amount of moral force available at a given point, and the effect, out of all proportion to its size, this same amount of moral force really produced when it was there. Surely you remember Thurber's Walter Mitty in his splendid vision of himself as a captain about to lead a desperate attack. Someone warns him of his situation: 'It's forty kilometers through hell!' And Mitty says softly, 'After all, what isn't?'

Today we have a way of praising ourselves for our compassion and for the courage of our candor. We are, to be sure, impatient with injustice and lack of concern for the disadvantaged. Thank God this is so. But concern for others does not exonerate us from the hard task of governing ourselves and renouncing the sleazy moral relativism best satirized by the comment of a famous writer that we should not be too hard on one of his contemporaries who 'only lies when he is very tired.'

As for our candor, our delight in no bluff and no pretense, in our calling a spade a spade—we have a lot of that. Nothing shocks us into silence, and to blush is to be square. The stuffy age of timid reticence is gone. Indeed, it now requires no particular courage to tell all the garbage that is on what we choose to call our minds. But candor is, even so, a two-way street. If down one side of it we fearlessly parade our lust, our four-letter words, and all of ourselves turned inside out for all to see, we have another obligation. And this obligation is to declare unashamedly the good we do prefer, the standards we do honor, the loyalties we do serve. Every college campus I know has far too many who are unwilling to stand up and be counted for what they really believe. This is the missing thing. And if it is missing in the fifth year a lot else will be missing also.

The third wish is for a belief in law. The adjustment of life to law, and of law to life may well be the enduring task of this generation. What a chance some dramatist now has to give his own account of present tensions in a new version of the Antigone story. For we are re-enacting that play of Sophocles. In the old drama Antigone by night buries the body of her dead brother against the edict of Creon, the king. The clash is between the law of the state and the higher human law to which Antigone feels herself bound. And so now we are in the thick of the question of civil disobedience, human rights and property rights, and what men feel are conflicting freedoms. Moreover, in America our problem is compounded by the tensions between federal and state law, by the hard constitutional questions that tore Abraham Lincoln's heart and were the subject of his last cabinet meeting on the very day of his death. Demonstrators, for example, accused by their detractors of breaking a local law, believe they are affirming another more commanding law.

This is no occasion to air the civil rights controversy. My mail is hot on both sides. If I did the many conflicting things I am asked to do I would be a peeled onion for sure. Some of these matters involve principle; some are solely matters of judgment and method. One wishes this distinction might be more widely recognized.

Who in his right mind would not prefer the ideal of Athenian democracy, with its reliance on discussion and deliberation rather than on marchings and demonstrations and sit-ins? I am sure that any intelligent man who marches would prefer it. But the world of Athens tolerated human conditions that humanity will now not tolerate. And to that degree Athens is no perfect model, except as a method.

This method should not go silently out of mind. For to this method we shall surely return and should return with, to use a phrase, 'all deliberate speed.' Meantime the present tensions have their creative use. They make some things appallingly clear: that nothing under Heaven is going to stop the realization in America of a desegregated society. And the full reign of law that we covet, laws in America, federal or state, will have honor and effect only if they rest on 'no substance less enduring than the human heart' and on an adequate concept of human life.

Let us hope and work for that clearance of men's dispositions which will give to law the base it should have. Meantime, let us not forget that the built-in problem of all civil disobedience is this—that any man, believing he has heard the right voices or seen his special light from the sky, can assert his right to take the law in his own hands. Bad men, as well as good men, can hear voices, and ultimately it may be you they want to take into their own hands. When all men feel they can play games with the law what you have is anarchy.

Six hundred years ago Jacopone da Todi made this remarkable prayer: 'O Thou who lovest me—set this love in order.' That is a prayer for the fifth year. There is ahead of us a great work of cleansing and renewal, but there is also a great work of living architecture called the law. This structure, rightly ordered, can be nobler than any building we shall make of brick or stone. It will be the guarantee of any freedom we will have.

The fourth wish is easier, since it is a private matter and can be quickly stated. It arises from the belief that a man or woman does well to find one thing he or she can really know and make a possession. This is something outside our business or profession that gives a 'quality to our idleness.' To know one thing and know it well tones up our whole existence in a world where we too often seem to be running to catch the last train. The range of possibilities, moreover, is very wide—an idea, a man or a place, a moment in history, a problem in science or creative work in the arts. The new instruments are all at hand to help us—the paper books, the fine recordings, the run of the whole natural world. One of the great aims of education, surely, is to make us aware of the enormous difference between 'time to live and time to kill.'

A belief in what is human, in courage, in law, and in the avocation of knowing one thing well. What is the fifth wish?

It is this—a belief that the fifth year is endless. In the distinguished conference held on our campus some six weeks ago, bringing together scholars from the East and the West, two striking insights emerged among many. They were a recurring awareness of the reality of the human self and, secondly, a recurring awareness that the time-bound, earth-bound self is not enough. We have an attachment to enduring things that far outsoar the shadows of our night. This instinct for immortality is no mere craving to keep alive the permanent possibility of sensation, to preserve our eating, drinking, getting-up-and-going-to-sleep self. This instinct for self-preservation—do you not feel it?—far transcends the instinct of a fly scurrying out of the way of some cosmic swatter.

Men have sought in many ways to believe in life beyond death —through analogies to nature, through philosophical argument, the mystic vision, or their own souls' invincible surmise. Some of

these insights are persuasive, but hardly objects for our critical
review this morning, for one is hardly likely to persuade any student that he is either logically or mystically immortal in the rush
of commencement weekend.

I do hope, however, that no senior is so unprofound that he
thinks a belief in personal immortality is not a matter of prime
importance. It is tremendously important. It makes a vast practical difference what one believes here. To believe that we can survive our death affects our entire measurement and estimation of
everything, the high risks we are likely to take, our whole perspective on the moral life—our actions, our responsibilities, our
loyalties. To pretend or feel indifference to this supreme question
is to proclaim a considerable shallowness of mind. For a Christian
to be indifferent to it is to make him as perfunctory as Edith Sit-
well's parrot who, when the family was gathered for prayers,
automatically covered his face with one claw.

What one decides finally, of course, is one's own business. And
the Christian knows that God can, if He choose, remain entirely
silent about the whole matter. But the Christian feels God did not
so choose—that there was, rather, a great Event in history and
that One who desired to live beyond His death did live. The
Christian Church arose out of one magnificent life to which was
given this shattering revelation about death. This, as it has been
said, was the news that ran around the Mediterranean world like
fire—that the God of illimitable love was also a God of power.
Men felt changed by this news. They could now mount up with
wings as eagles, they could walk and not faint, they could be
filled with all the fullness of God.

No moment in the four college years of this senior class will
probably be more remembered than that November afternoon of
their junior year when they learned that John F. Kennedy was
dead. Regardless of political affiliation, they felt on that day that
they had lost something of themselves. They had seen other
young men die—two of their own classmates, Martin Galloway
and Wayne Hinger, whom we think of this morning. This class

has felt in an almost incredible way the tragic sense of life. And thus the one thing I most want to say to them this morning is this, and on it I would bet my life: over these three young men death has no dominion. The night shall be light around them. And now they have no age at all. For the fifth year is endless.

# Second Finding
## (1966)

The members of the class that will be graduated tomorrow morning have carried a very heavy four-year burden. Since their first week as freshmen they have known that theirs would be the commencement of the Centennial Year. Whatever singularity this particular honor has, it clearly has its drawbacks. In the general welter of looking fore and aft, it's a little like being the last of a long line or the cut ribbon at the opening of a bridge. Moreover, ceremonial duties of the class of 1966 do not end tomorrow. Come the fiftieth reunion in the year 2016, the College will be marking its sesquicentennial year, and significance will be pursued once more. Some will arrive by spaceship from the outer galaxies. The food at the alumni dinner will be concentrated pills, and, one supposes, the class will listen to after-pellet speakers demonstrating the need of the alumni fund in the age of the two-cent dollar.

There should be a special pride in the class of 1966. For these have not been easy years for anybody who is young. World events, man's tiresome inhumanity to man, the aura of uncertainty in all planning, the questioning of fixed stars in the moral universe—all this is not a new story, but it is told in new dimensions and with louder sound effects. Moreover, it is now harder for a man even to relieve his feelings in strong language, for the alleged death of God has deprived his blasphemies of any force. The class of 1966 has had to be men for all seasons, who have done, on the whole, quite well. We are proud of them. And my comfort to any senior who is still troubled is the wry comment Robert Frost made on his sixtieth birthday in talking to the students at Amherst College. He scorned the notion that students were living in the most desperate of all ages. He said it was immodest for any man to think of himself as going down before the mightiest forces ever mobilized by God.

Our theme this morning comes from one of the best poems of Richard Wilbur, our delightful guest of a month ago. It is used with his permission, and even with his blessing. Several years ago I was much taken by his short poem, 'The Beautiful Changes.' 'Changes,' notice, is not a noun, but a verb. In swift and telling images the poem moves to its concluding statement: *

> —the beautiful changes
> In such kind ways,
> Wishing ever to sunder
> Things and things' selves for a second finding, to lose
> For a moment all that it touches back to wonder.

That phrase, 'the second finding,' has haunted me ever since. This morning, for a little while, I hope it may haunt you.

For it is a true account of what does happen to us—this moving from one ground to another; this losing for a moment one thing in order to find, in wonder, another thing, perhaps something recovered, something reappraised, something understood and now valued for the first time. Into such spiritual history, which I should suppose is the spiritual history of everybody in this room, is gathered the long story of our re-examinations, our renunciations, our recoveries, and our renewals. These, indeed, are our 'conversions'—and in far more than the religious sense. The 'sec-

---

* From "The Beautiful Changes," in *The Beautiful Changes* by Richard Wilber (New York: Harcourt, Brace & World, 1954). Reprinted by permission of the publisher.

ond findings' may be more than one. They are the key moments
in our minds and souls. They are important because they have
practical application for the decisions we have to make on the ur-
gent issues of our time.

All this is not to say that everything must change and that our
first findings are always wrong. Sometimes we hit it straight off,
like the old Maine sailor who used to say, 'I can tell a good ship
with a single blow of the eye.' Some cynics would say, that the
first findings are all that most of us ever get! Dean Inge once remarked that we are forever the person that we were in the
decade in which we were between twenty and thirty. And Scott
Fitzgerald was even more blunt than that: 'There are,' he said,
'no second acts in American lives.' But Justice Oliver Wendell
Holmes, who kept learning new things into his youthful nineties,
had a truer view: 'Once in a while a book or a hint or a phrase
gives one a shudder of doubt whether one needs to reconstruct
one's universe.' His long life was one of America's best efforts at
discovery and rediscovery, revision and reaffirmation.

The second findings come, of course, in great variety. A first
type comes as renunciation. For renunciation of some kind is often
the prelude to creation. Men do, in this world, 'scorn delights,
and live laborious days.' They give up this to inherit that. There
have been many arguments against giving oneself over to sensuality and incontinence, and Cicero's is surely one of the most
penetrating and unusual: that if you give yourself up to sensuality,
you will soon find yourself unable to think of anything else. The
price you pay isn't just some violation of a moral law, but the
surrender of all the rest of a rich and meaningful world. Some
things, as the poet said, cost not less than everything. We can
drown in excess. One evening, long ago, it was my pleasure to
take the late Desmond MacCarthy, the fine dramatic critic of the
London Sunday *Times*, to the theater on his first night in America. Coming out, after the play, we saw, he for the first time, the

dazzling lights of Broadway. He blinked at them awhile and, turning to me, said, 'Tell me, how do you Americans ever manage to celebrate anything!' It was a nice point.

Surely American history has no nobler exhibit than the second finding that Robert E. Lee made after his own surrender. On a September afternoon of 1865, after a three-day journey on Traveller, the horse that had carried him through the war, Lee rode, a dejected yet dignified man, into Lexington, Virginia, to take up his new duties as the president of the college that now bears Washington's name and his own. The insignia were all removed from his gray uniform, all the bright buttons cut away. Quietly he began his great work of reconciliation, telling young southerners, who came hot-headed to the campus, to forget the past and grow up now to their new country. Lee would never read anything whatever about the war. His chief books were the Bible, the Book of Common Prayer, and the *Iliad*, in which he must have lingered long over Homer's awareness that 'the gods have appointed an enduring heart to the children of men.' One day, when he was on his last visit to northern Virginia, a young mother brought her child to Lee to ask his blessing. Lee took the little baby in his arms, looked at it, then turned to the mother and said, very slowly and thoughtfully, 'Teach him he must deny himself.' Beyond all the battles, this is the Lee that men will remember.

There is, of course, the second finding that comes, not with renouncement, but with revision. This comes of the critical power that moves us to a higher level of choice. I mean, not just the new knowledge, but all the third- and fourth-rate stuff that shrieks for our attention. Douglass Woodruff, in a debate at the Oxford Union, once ironically complimented his opponent on his oratory. 'As I listened to him,' Woodruff said, 'I seemed to see, behind his shoulder, the ghost of Gladstone giving him ghostly advice, and the shade of Disraeli, giving him shady advice.' We get a lot of both kinds, and sometimes it isn't easy to tell the difference. Much of it comes

> In books that are as altars where we kneel
> To consecrate the flicker, not the flame!

Yet daily about us we see men and women trying, with reason and imagination, to think and feel their way to the higher ground and the second finding.

There is also, beyond renunciation and revision, the way of re-affirmation—the repossession of what we already know or have. One thinks here of the suggestion in Horace that the end of all our lives is simply to become what we are. When the familiar becomes wonderful again at the touch of new insights and associations that the years and the mind bring to it—when what we knew only as bloodless abstractions acquire embodiment; when poetry becomes poems, and art becomes pictures, and music the tunes of glory we heard so often in this very place this year, there is a new and deeper affirmation. We see a Churchill raise a reckless courage that won him nothing but the scorn of his critics to the high valor of 1940. We see Wordsworth endowing the English Lakes with the beauty of his imagination, as I wish somebody someday would endow Wayne County. One remembers Thornton Wilder's turning the life of Grover's Corners into an existence beyond price when all the little things became important. We see the sheer cleverness of Bernard Shaw raised to profound beauty and insight when in *Saint Joan* 'he stumbled upon a subject larger than himself.' John Mason Brown used to say, 'Her conquest of Mr. Shaw must be counted among her major victories.' Albert Schweitzer, for example, sees multiple genius raised to exalted service at the touch of two chapters of the Gospel of St. Matthew: 'Heal the sick, cleanse the lepers—take my yoke upon you, for my yoke is easy and the burden is light.' C. S. Lewis works out from agnosticism into a reasoned belief in immortality. But his second finding that turned belief into certainty in these matters wasn't based on reason at all, but came through the death of one man he knew, Charles Williams—whom it was my own high privilege to know. Mr. Lewis put it very simply: 'When the idea of death and the idea of Charles Williams thus met in my mind, it was the idea of death that was changed.'

All men—not just the gifted and the great—know the second findings that touch things back to wonder. Our lives are rich in this common glory. The fragment of a song after many years, a voice or face recalled, the well-remembered place on land or water, the night sky above the desert or the sea, a child's innocence or an old man's quiet—any of these will serve. And not all is recollection. The second findings arise from something newly ventured or discerned. They can be either affirmation or reaffirmation, when 'day unto day uttereth speech, and night unto night showeth knowledge.' There is another name for them, of course. They can be our salvation.

Thus far I have been speaking of the spirit's changes or of what Henry More might have called the 'rise and fall of life in the soul of man.' Let us think now of practical affairs—of what has to happen in the world in 1966 and thereafter. The second findings needed there are crucial now. And our graduates tomorrow are going to be involved in them.

The finding of peace is the first—of peace and some world order. We have already the patterns and framework of peace. We have known them for a long time. But the will to it and the disposition for it in the working majority of mankind is quite another matter. In a world where 25 per cent of the human race owns 75 per cent of the wealth, somebody is going to be asked about this. Not by the Communists. The Communists don't ask; they tell you. But history is going to ask: 'When you, for the first time, at last had the practical means of making the necessities of life attainable for mankind, what did you do about it?' Here is our chance, at last, of our finding what William James called the moral equivalent of war—something we can put our hands to, with ardor. And no bumbling on our part, no muttering that the poor nations prefer their poverty or that you can't love those who don't want to be loved—none of these excuses will ever be sufficient.

I believe that, far this side of pacifism, far this side of any disavowal of private enterprise, far this side of loose economic views that are as 'casual as a bride's personal checking account,' we can be decent, concerned people who are determined to spend a better balance of our wealth in the pursuits of peace and human betterment than ever now we manage to do. Lord David Cecil used to say, 'Barbarism is not behind us, but beneath us.' And he wasn't talking about the enemy. We have so far to go in the way of down-to-earth intelligent love. And every dinosaur in every museum, as has been noted many times, is a warning to us of what happens when we plunge about fast without the use of our brains. Brains just could be one second finding.

Barbara Ward reminds us of Professor Buckminster Fuller's view that 'the most rational way actually of considering the whole human race today is to see it as the ship's crew of a single spaceship on which all of us, with a remarkable combination of security and vulnerability, are making our pilgrimage through infinity. . . . This space voyage is totally precarious. . . . We are a ship's company on a small ship. Rational behavior is the condition of survival.' Our task, of course, is to 'turn a mob,' which is what we are now, 'into a community.' *

Miss Ward believes that 'when the astronauts spin through more than a dozen sunrises and sunsets in a single day and night; when the whole globe lies below them with California one moment and Japan the next; when, as they return from space they feel spontaneously, with the first Soviet spaceman: "how beautiful it is, our earth." ' . . . 'what may we not expect,' she asks, 'from

* Barbara Ward, *Spaceship Earth* (New York: Columbia University Press, 1966).

men whose habitat is increasingly the heavens and who learn to see the earth as, today, we see the moon?'

When Columbus made landfall in a new continent, Miss Ward reminds us, the Middle Ages were over. 'Changes on stupendous scales do not leave the human imagination untouched. They cannot fail to change the whole context and significance of petty terrestrial squabbles.'

To find peace and order on so grand a scale depends partly on another second finding nearer home—a new sense for human worth and a regard for it, in spite of all the crowds and technics of our time. Not just a regard for the underprivileged and the victims of prejudice. It is easy to be a professional liberal and 'professionally' love mankind. And it's especially easy to be a professional conservative and 'professionally' love only the people who have earned the right to be loved. The harder thing is to love somebody just because you love him, without any premeditation, without any calculation, and with something of Schweitzer's spontaneous reverence for life. Hilaire Belloc tells of his friend, James Allison, whose cow strayed into a neighbor's yard. (This may well be the homeliest illustration ever used in a baccalaureate address, but I can't resist it because it cuts deep.) The neighbor came running to James Allison and said, 'That cow poked its head in at my window. Imagine my feelings!' Whereupon Allison replied, 'Imagine the cow's feelings!' Someday our second finding in sympathy and awareness may have to go as far as that.

All the second findings we have been thinking about this morning—whether for the individual or for society—are deeply related to our view of the world or to the faith we hold. Faith itself, indeed, is full of second findings. It can be formal and casual, or it can be alive, be what Arthur Compton said it was, 'the best we know, on which we would willingly bet our lives.'

For we are asked to make choices—choices we often wish we

might postpone or evade. As W. H. Auden and others have shown, we are invited now to something several cuts better than the dreary dialogue of 'ourselves about ourselves' and to something far exceeding the 'liberty of escaped slaves.'

For the Christian there is a great likelihood now of a second finding because we have revived, in a striking way, the old debate between faith and works. It has always seemed to me a false antithesis. Surely the one passes into and informs the other. Faith grows hollow when nothing is done about it and needs something good to work at to be real. On the other hand, good works alone can become, if uninformed by faith, just another kind of secular humanism. But not necessarily! For there is an ancient promise: 'He that doeth the will of the Father shall know of the doctrine, whether it be of God.' In short, something else may happen. And, conversely, the man of faith may feel some stirring to put his shoulder to the wheel. It's a new step either way, open to all.

If a man wants to know what God is he is most likely to find out by looking at Him in the life of His beloved Son. It has been this way for a long time. Paul knew a shining light and a voice on the Damascus road—at his second finding. He knew, not so much what, but Whom he had believed. For sometimes we do not do the finding at all. Sometimes we are found.

# The Apprentice's Secret
## (1967)

Photographers have a sleek and devious way of posing four or five otherwise innocent people round a table and putting something in the hands of one of them that looks like a vital document. The whole group then concentrates on that poor piece of paper as if it were a large check or Magna Carta. The steady gazers in this hoax may be corporation directors, the officers of a women's club planning a bazaar, or college presidents plotting to take their kingdom of excellence by violence. The false and surely self-conscious piece of paper may be anything at all—a blank sheet, a page ripped from a seed catalogue, or an ad for Bab-O. But it draws profound and riveted attention. The whole process has always seemed to me a delightful masterpiece of irrelevance and collective phoniness.

Tomorrow morning we place in some three hundred hands a document that carries far more meaning. Sheep gave their lives for it. It is now signed and sealed. Seniors stayed up late for it. And the prospect of it is, of course, what brings us together on this baccalaureate morning. For four years it has been pursued—by some who take their honors in talented stride, by some who traveled a harder road and whose attainment marks some very real and quiet spiritual triumph, by some who had to use a microscope to find the required points for graduation. As I saw some of them anxiously flipping the pages of the catalogue—perhaps for the first time in their undergraduate lives—I was reminded of the old legend about W. C. Fields, whose way of life was more buoyant than it was regular. A friend found him bedfast with a severe illness and reading the Bible for dear life. The surprised friend said, 'You—doing that?' The bloodshot eyes looked up and the weary voice replied, 'I'm looking for loopholes!'

Anyhow, we're glad they made it, by whatever road they came. And this morning we welcome their fathers and mothers, their families and friends on this distinctly family occasion and share your rightful pride in them. Tomorrow, we well realize, marks a culmination of plans and hopes and even sacrifice begun long ago—of risks taken, of faith justified. The times are not easy on the young; and, come to think of it, the young are not always easy on the times. After four years we hope you like them as well as we do. And if there's some little thing that startles you— something about their looks, their hair, or their present opinions that doesn't quite jibe with your own views—we suggest you remember Coleridge's observation that young people possessing anything like perfect taste merely reflected the lack of real talent.

This morning, as the class of 1967 stands for a little while at the still point that separates the Ivory Tower from what they choose to believe is the real world, we invite you to think for a moment of a somewhat homely but I hope deeply important baccalaureate theme. The infelicitous title, with its awkward sibilants, reminds me somehow of the tough time I always have in pronouncing the word 'forsythia.' But hold that not too hardly against us. For the apprentice and his secret are important symbols and touch the very center of our lives. Our theme is this: that all good and happy men and women are apprentices, who will and should remain so to the end of their lives. And the purpose of education is to produce them.

The apprentice is old in history. Laws concerning him appear in the Code of Hammurabi. The training of a skilled craftsman at the hands of a master workman is an ancient form of the tutorial relationship—where the teacher-student ratio is one to one. There was always a firm contract. With the English guilds of the Middle Ages the term of indenture was seven years. The apprentice was given the necessities of life while he did the work that meant the learning of his trade. He frequently lived in the master's house. Often he married the master's daughter, thus doubling the dose of paternalism he received. His pay started when he became a journeyman.

Contrary to what you might think, the apprentice system still survives, all over the world, and not just among impoverished medical interns in hospitals and the dedicated slaves in our summer theaters. In 1934 the Bureau of Apprenticeship was set up in the United States Department of Labor. This bureau now lists some three hundred apprenticable occupations. And although only one in ten skilled workers now comes from apprentice programs, there were in January 1963, some 158,000 registered apprentices. The number is declining. Modern apprenticeship tends to occur in trade school classes, in co-operative education, and in on-the-job training. We need far more of it, especially when there is human displacement by automation.

Whatever the outward facts, many skeptics will loudly proclaim that the spirit of apprenticeship is gone. All we have, they say, are young men and women in a hurry who would much prefer to arrive than to travel hopefully. They go gimlet-eyed for the quick returns. And everybody wants to be the boss straight-off. Time and the long river of experience have nothing to do with the matter. Today we do not float; we fly. In his satire on British Philistinism a century ago, Matthew Arnold reminds us of Mrs. Gooch's Golden Rule, or the Divine Injunction, 'Be Ye Perfect,' done into British—the sentence Sir Daniel Gooch said his mother repeated to him every morning when he was a boy going to work: 'Ever remember, my dear Dan, that you should look forward to being some day manager of that concern!' The modern Mrs. Gooch would delete 'look forward' and 'someday' and

say, 'Dan, cream it now!' She would tick off the whole dry run
of guaranteed raises, escalation clauses, fringe benefits, vacation
pay, and stabilized coffee breaks—with a kind of insistence on industrial predestination that would put even a Presbyterian to
shame. And she would be overlooking one prime fact about Dan
—that for all his bright eyes and eager hands, he may still be only
half-baked.

Such, at any rate, runs the skeptical generalization about our
young men in a hurry. And there is truth in it, to be sure. But I
know too many young men and women taking the slow, hard
road, modest about themselves, willing to take large time out of
their lives in service to others, to believe the spirit of apprenticeship is gone forever. Many young people I know have sensed its
vital secret. They face up to the rigorous training required of
them. They want to earn what they expect to receive.

The true apprentice was a lucky fellow, with many blessings.
Under contract, he knew discipline and law. If he were under a
skilled and humane master worker, he had a sense of security
along with a growing competence. For the very word 'apprentice' comes from an old French word meaning 'to learn,' 'to lay
hold of with the mind.' And this 'learning' was his secret—and his
joy—with its overtones of direction, movement, hope, and life.
He was not a person standing still, settling merely for what is—
three-parts iced-over and growing older by the hour. He saw far
horizons, and something of the poet's intimation that

> whether we be young or old,
> Our destiny, our being's heart and home,
> Is with infinitude, and only there;
> With hope it is, hope that can never die,
> Effort, and expectation, and desire,
> And something evermore about to be.
>                         (Wordsworth, *The Prelude*)

In short, the apprentice's secret was life.

It was no mean secret, and the aim of education is to put it in a man's heart so it lasts him all his days. We have never assumed here that a senior with a diploma is an educated man. Who, indeed, ever is? He is a potentially educated man, who knows how to continue his education to the very end of his life. He has ways of doing this. Thus, as ongoing apprentice, he may have life instead of that internal aging, that death of the mind and spirit which can come before one dies—adventure, hope, wonder, and movement gone. He knows how to put in new crops from time to time 'to preserve the soil' and avoid 'ruinous erosion.'

It was once my pleasure, when I was working for a publisher, to try to get Alfred North Whitehead, the mathematician and philosopher, to do a book on Wordsworth. This he longed to do, but felt he could not, in the light of all the other mounting plans he had. I have told some of you before of the winter day in Cambridge when I saw an old man coming along Brattle Street, bent over with the years; as we passed I suddenly realized it was Mr. Whitehead, his face radiant with youth and inquiry and an ongoing apprenticeship, even when he was already in so many ways the master.

The spirit of apprenticeship is not just something it is nicer to have as a quickening force in our lives. It is rather our inevitable condition, make what we will of it. For, whether we like it or not, we are all apprentices. This our permanent assignment in a world that will always outrun even our keenest minds and the highest levels of our competence. Though we be 'encased in talents like a uniform,' our talent is never enough. And it's always the best people who know the inevitable distance between what could be and what is. No man probably writes better than E. B. White, but English usage, he once reminded us, is not just a matter of mere taste, judgment, and education—but sometimes 'sheer luck, like getting across the street.' Even William Shakespeare felt the divine discontent, 'desiring this man's art, and that man's scope.'

In our world of expanding knowledge we turn in desperation

to the expert but the collective experts can't save us. For, as Harold Laski once said in a brilliant essay on their limitations, 'the expert tends to make his subject the measure of life, instead of making life the measure of his subject,' thus confusing 'learning with wisdom.' We step up our sophistication and lose the freshness of our earlier world. Then we start over. I shall never forget the afternoon in Princeton when I heard Bruno Walter, at the height of his powers, rehearsing a group of highly trained singers in the superb chorale of Bach's *St. Matthew Passion*. He rapped his baton and then, in words I wish were recorded, asked for something better than he was getting. He praised the singers for their talent and training. But he said, in effect, 'The really great singing of music like this is congregational singing.' He then gave his memories of a little church in Germany where he heard singing as a boy. 'You trained people know how to get all the effects, all the striking heights and depths, in brilliant contrast. But this is simpler and profounder than that. Sing it as the congregation sang it when you were young. Now let us try it again!' Once more they were all apprentices and sang that chorale as I have never heard it sung, except by some of your sons and daughters as apprentices, in this very chapel. And, remembering, I think of the great lines from the *Four Quarters*: *

> We shall not cease from exploration
> And the end of all our exploring
> Will be to arrive where we started
> And know the place for the first time . . .
>           here, now, always—
> A condition of complete simplicity
> (Costing not less than everything).

Our inevitable and permanent role as apprentices should keep us humble, but it should exalt and not depress us. The endless knowledge that weighs upon us, should engender in us no despair.

* From "Little Gidding," in *Four Quartets* by T. S. Eliot (New York: Harcourt, Brace & World, 1943). Reprinted by permission of the publisher.

We should not enact the old Savoyard proverb, 'There are so many things to do that I think I'll go back to bed.' There is much within our power—a competence we can attain, great themes we can isolate and enrich by experience, many breakthroughs we can make. We can push our outposts into the darkness, 'establishing no post, not perfectly in light and firm.' It is still possible to leave our campsites better than we found them. But we do all this more effectively—and it's more fun—if the apprentice's secret and his spirit are in our hearts. What we should not resemble is the professor who asked his college president for a raise in salary, saying, 'After all, I've had twenty years' experience.' To which the president was forced to reply, 'You haven't had twenty years' experience. You've had the same experience twenty times.'

There are specific areas of our common life right now—areas in which we are still apprentices—where the lively spirit of the apprentice himself is sorely needed. Everyone could make his own list of these. There are the still-beckoning frontiers of medicine and science, of social justice, of population control, the production and distribution of goods, the enigmas of automation, our whole political tone and structure, the clearing of the air we breathe, the vexing problems of education, the nation's biggest business. An American philosopher once asked what were our country's two unique contributions to the world. He quickly named mass production and the idea of the federal union of states on a mass scale. Would you join me in adding a third, provided we can pull it off: mass education, the education of all our citizenry, with high quality? In all these areas there is exciting and healthy ferment—and an incredible need.

We are apprentices also in other areas of special significance—in the bringing, for example, of critical and informed choice to our lives, that we can, among the welter of things and stimuli that surround us, know the modulation of desire. I hope some of you know Professor D. J. Boorstin's book, *The Image, or What Happened to the American Dream*. It is a devastating account of 'how we have used our wealth, our literacy, our technology, and our progress, to create the thicket of unreality which stands between us and the facts of life.' He elaborates the 'illusions which flood our experience' because of our extravagant expectations. We expect too much of the world. 'We expect our house not only to shelter us, to keep us warm in winter and cool in summer, but to relax us, to dignify us, to encompass us with soft music and interesting hobbies, to be a playground, a theater, and a bar. We expect our two-week vacation to be romantic, exotic, cheap, and effortless. . . . We expect new heroes every season, a literary masterpiece every month, a dramatic spectacular every week, a rare sensation every night. We expect everybody to feel free to disagree . . . yet not to rock the boat. . . . We expect anything and everything. We expect the contradictory and the impossible —far more than the world can offer.' Somewhere, somebody must learn how to choose.

We are apprentices at giving form and heightening to experience—through art and music and literature, that we may know the dimensions of wonder and awe, what Goethe called 'the best part of our lives.' 'Stripped of their poetry,' Aldous Huxley once wrote, 'the plots of all the world's great tragedies are simply items from the front page of the *Police Gazette*.' We have become apprentices at supplying the poetry which arises when 'noble natures, eminently gifted,' attain to the high level of that wonder and awe.

We are apprentices at service to our fellow men, for all our community endeavors and the devotion of many hands. The other day I went through the slum area of a great city that overwhelms the imagination—a tragic amateur night at the great theater of our own humanity. And the pursuit of peace continues to be the painful inch-by-inch bartering we have all learned to engage in, lacking in imagination because we follow the old tired ways that conceive of peace merely as the absence of war. A very great man whom it was my privilege to talk with not long ago— he is as down-to-earth as any man I know and shrewdly handles large practical affairs—suddenly broke across our conversation and cried out with fervor, 'The rare and missing quality in every phase of the life I know is imagination.' We are still apprentices at that. For lack of it we inch our painful way.

The apprentice often lived, you will recall, in the master's house. And this is, of course, the great question about any of us, too. Where do we think we live? For our view of the world is the final, determining thing about us. Are we the blind product of some blind and senseless happening long ago? The evolving consciousness out of nowhere? The fallen spirits from some once high place? The insulted and the injured? The abandoned and forgotten? The brief traveler between two oblivions? Or are we the meaningful sons of God on whom His love has been placed eternally? What do we think of Christ? Who do we say He is? Is our apprenticeship in the world some lonely, meaningless struggle? Or, do we live in the Master's house?

We have never asked any student here to tell us his private answer to these questions. There are no tests of faith for graduation. And on this baccalaureate morning there is no stampede in these high matters. Any group of three hundred students will reflect many varieties of religious experience—honest question, real or assumed indifference, faith and commitment. These matters are not settled always by graduation. But one does somehow suspect the intelligence of anybody who, by that time, thinks these things are of no account. President Pusey, of Harvard, a place not commonly thought of as a provincial, church-related college, lays it straight on the line. 'It would seem to me that the finest fruit of serious learning should be the ability to speak the word God without reserve or embarrassment, certainly without adolescent resentment; rather with some sense of communion, with reverence and with joy.'

I would go farther than that. Any thoughtful person who has kept even his eyes and ears open—let alone his heart—within the context of a Christian culture must, in the name of his own good wits, sometime and at some point in his journey ask himself, 'Do I

or do I not live in the Master's house?' For the answer, if yes, is
the ultimate dimension in the apprentice's secret. For then he
knows his works and days are of some new and enduring account.
And he thinks of himself, not as some senseless minnow in the
cosmic creek, but as one of the sons of God. He is himself included in the immense language of eternal love. 'If I take the
wings of the morning, and dwell in the uttermost parts of the sea,
even there shall thy hand lead me, and thy right hand shall hold
me.' 'Even the night shall be light about me.'

There is no ambiguity about that kind of relationship between
apprentice and Master: 'I am the true vine, and my Father is the
husbandman.' 'Abide in me and I in you.' 'I am the vine, ye are
the branches.' 'As the Father hath loved me, so have I loved you;
continue ye in my love.' 'And when the Spirit of Truth is come,
He will guide you into all truth.'

And then it is the apprentice knows a new indenture—the high
partnership with very God Himself in the ongoing work of creation. He can say, and mean it, the great prayer of St. Augustine,
who himself knew all the checkered and labyrinthine ways that
lead men home. It is the prayer of all the apprentices of God:

> Let us not leave Thee alone to make in the secret of Thy
> knowledge, as Thou didst before the creation of the firma-
> ment, the division of light from darkness; let the children of
> Thy Spirit, placed in their firmament, make their light shine
> upon the earth, mark the division of night and day, and an-
> nounce the revolution of the times; for the old order is passed,
> and the new arises. The night is spent, and the day is come
> forth.

*Ladies and Gentlemen of the Class of 1967:*

Sir Winston Churchill served a lifetime of inspired apprentice-
ships. He would tackle anything—soldiering, politics, writing,
speaking, state-craft, bricklaying, and painting. He knew colossal
failures on more than one occasion. Then he came to the shining
hour when he saved the whole free world. His aunt once said of

him, 'You can easily discover all Winston's faults in an hour. But you can spend the rest of your life discovering his virtues.'

This morning we say nothing about your faults, provided you have any. But we expect that, as the years go by, many will be discovering your virtues. This morning we salute that bright potential and express again our pride in you.

Robert Frost once said that if you had to love something you could do worse than give your heart to a college. How quaint that seems in the light of what is now good academic practice. It is bad form now to love a college. You are supposed to love the abstract things—like truth, and freedom and justice. But not a little piece of earth, or the homely memories of the changing seasons, or the times you had or the people you knew. No one is supposed to put roots down or have the sentiment of belonging. So it is said. You've read all the articles that say it.

You may be in for some surprises on this score. This is a place

> Rich in the faith of thousands living,
> Proud of the deeds of thousands dead.

They were men and women with just as many good brains as you. For belonging has its apprenticeship, too. Unashamedly, this morning I express the hope that you will belong here. It will be good for Wooster, and it just may be good for you. At least the house will be always open.

And our prayer for you this morning is an old one: that the Lord may bless you and keep you, that He may make His face to shine upon you and be gracious unto you, that He may lift up the light of His countenance upon you and give you peace.